Hegel's Recollection

SUNY Series in Hegelian Studies
Quentin Lauer, Editor

Hegel's Recollection

A STUDY OF IMAGES IN THE
Phenomenology of Spirit

Donald Phillip Verene
PROFESSOR OF PHILOSOPHY
EMORY UNIVERSITY

State University of New York Press
Albany

Published by
State University of New York Press, Albany

For information, address State University of New York
Press, State University Plaza, Albany, N.Y., 12246

Library of Congress Cataloging in Publication Data

Verene, Donald Phillip, 1937–
  Hegel's recollection.

  (SUNY series in Hegelian studies)
  Includes index.
  1. Hegel, Georg Wilhelm Friedrich, 1770–1831.
Phänomenologie des Geistes. 2. Spirit. 3. Conscience.
4. Truth. 5. Metaphor. 6. Irony. 7. Imagination.
I. Title. II. Series.
B2929.V47 1985   193   84–26884
ISBN 0–88706–011–0
ISBN 0–88706–012–9 (pbk.)

10 9 8 7 6 5 4 3 2 1

For Ernesto Grassi
In friendship

Contents

If this essay had to do with such artifice, these words should not have been allowed to enter right from the start; but like the cabinet minister in a comedy, they should have been required to walk around throughout the whole play in an overcoat, unbuttoning it only in the last scene, allowing the star of wisdom to flash forth.

Hegel, *Wer denkt abstrakt?* (1807)

Preface

Hegel had an extraordinary command of metaphor and irony as well as a deeply rational mind. In his major writings Hegel employs these powerful tropes together with the discursive statement of his philosophy. We have only to think of the much-quoted owl of Minerva metaphor from the preface to the *Philosophy of Right* or the assertion that the true is a bacchanalian revel from the preface to the *Phenomenology of Spirit* to realize that Hegel combines the great discursive power of his thought with an equally great rhetorical power of expression. What Hegel says in his philosophy is extraordinary and how he says it is equally extraordinary. We have become so accustomed to regarding the rhetorical elements in a philosopher's thought as mere embellishments that we read right past them. Later we may use the philosopher's metaphors as keys to recall the meanings of his doctrine without a very clear awareness of the role these are playing in giving us access to the thinker's thoughts.

Hegel himself had no real interest in the imagination as a philosophical concern nor had he interest in rhetoric as a philosophical problem. Yet Hegel, like other great thinkers in the classical and modern world, used imagination and rhetorical speech as a method to convey basic meanings of his thought. In Hegel's work this is especially true of the *Phenomenology of Spirit*. It is a work of vast imaginative and rational structure, a colossus without equal in modern philosophy. The *Phenomenology of Spirit* is usually understood purely in discursive terms. Hegel's metaphors and ironies are appreciated as clever instruments and are treated by Hegel's commentators as if they were purely conceptual ideas.

Hegel is the philosopher of the concept, the concrete concept *(Begriff)*, and thus anything said about his work that is not conceptual in tone seems questionable. When Hegel has made the concept itself concrete, imaginative speech seems unnecessary. Fundamental to Hegel's philosophy is that the concept should be understood in its own terms; content and form are to come together in the concrete concept. Commentary on Hegel traditionally focuses on the concept and on the language of the concept, which is discursive. When we come to Hegel's works we hunt the concept. To

ix

speak about Hegel's imagination seems strange to us. He is a conceptual thinker and we must understand the concept discursively and concretely.

Much of Hegel's work, I think, especially the *Science of Logic* and its shorter version in the *Encyclopaedia,* can be approached in these terms. But the *Phenomenology of Spirit,* Hegel's "voyage of discovery," can be approached differently. In the *Phenomenology* there is a struggle between imagistic or pictorial ways of thinking and the concept. In this work Hegel is struggling to give the concept birth. This struggle is one of passing through the image to the concept, moving from a language of appearance to a language of reality. In this process *Bild* and *Begriff* work dialectically against each other. This opposition within Hegel's philosophical doctrine is also present in Hegel's manner of writing.

The *Phenomenology* is organized through a number of master metaphors and ironic twists of meaning—the pun on *das Meinen,* with which Hegel begins the work, the inverted or topsy-turvy world, the master and servant, the unhappy consciousness, Hegel's ironic treatment of phrenology, the spiritual animal kingdom, the beautiful soul, the image of the divine with which Hegel closes the work. These are only some of Hegel's master metaphors and ironies which are employed in the *Phenomenology.* Through such tropes we encounter the rational movement of the concept; we encounter Hegel's philosophical ideas themselves—the in-itself, the for-itself, the transformation of substance into subject, consciousness, experience, absolute spirit, to mention only a few. We have access to the "science of the experience of consciousness," as Hegel calls his work in the preface to the *Phenomenology,* through both our powers of metaphorical under-standing and our powers of discursive thought. Hegel uses both these powers to achieve his meaning and we must give attention to both if we are to understand it.

Hegel's *Phenomenology* has been so strongly approached in discursive terms that I wish to begin on the other side of his thought and to bring forth aspects of this work that have been missed in its discursive treatment. It is not my purpose to approach Hegel's thought simply in terms of its imaginative dimension. This would be equally one-sided in the opposite direction. Instead I wish to ask what can be learned of Hegel's ideas if we approach them with an interest in the meaning of his metaphors, images, and ironies. Approached in this way, Hegel's thought appears in a new perspective; aspects of its meaning appear that can appear in no other way.

In this book I have selected several leading sections of the *Phenomenology.* The titles of these parts of the *Phenomenology* are the basis of the chapter titles of my work. Other parts of the *Phenomenology* could have been selected; the parts on which this book is based are intended as only representative. They particularly lend themselves to my thesis and they are parts of Hegel's work which have interested me personally. In the twenty years that have passed since I first taught the *Phenomenology* these sections have haunted my memory. Ideas about their meaning have come back to me again and again and in this sense the principle of selection I have used is personal. This book is not a series of independent commentaries on these sections of Hegel's work. Throughout my specific views runs a general perspective on the meaning of the *Phenomenology*. Because the true is the whole, I have found that there must be a general view of the meaning of Hegel's work present in order to articulate the meaning of any one of its sections.

This work is not an introduction to Hegel's *Phenomenology*. It presupposes a familiarity with Hegel's text and is itself a recollection of what is there. Unlike many traditional commentaries, this work does not set out "to prove something." The attempt to prove something, to present the authoritative interpretation, can offer precise and interesting knowledge of many points, but such interpretation also closes the text off from us. My approach has been to open the text up, to see it with new eyes. Such an approach is vulnerable. I expect it may be said that I have not presented the "real" Hegel. But the reader must judge for himself what may be learned of Hegel or Hegelianism as a living form of thought in these pages. I offer the reader my version of the ladder with which the ascent of consciousness can be attempted.

I do not regard the views I express to be exactly what Hegel himself meant. Nor do I intend what I say here to be simply my own philosophical view imposed upon Hegel's work. My approach falls between these two. In each chapter I have sought to uncover ideas that are within the text, but which, once uncovered, do not always point to what we have come to expect the text to mean. They are ideas that often lead out in their own directions. Uncovering these ideas allows us to look at Hegel differently and can allow us to raise in a new way the question: what is living and what is dead in Hegel?

At a period in which the pendulum of interest in Hegel swings strongly in the direction of his *Logic,* the present study is a statement of the importance and liveliness of the *Phenomenology*. The present study is intended more as a projective work than as a definitive interpretation. It takes seriously that the true is the bacchanalian revel at which not a member is sober. Hegel invites the reader to participate in his work, not just to think about what it says but to think with it, to extend it and bring it to life. If we cannot place ourselves in the work, we become mere technicians of its interpretation. We must be able to think thoughts freely with Hegel and risk something of our own philosophical ability on behalf of our understanding. Without life philosophy goes nowhere.

It is likely that my theme in this work will be misunderstood. It may be thought that I am claiming that Hegel's fundamental interest is in the image and not the concept. This is not my claim. Hegel is fundamentally concerned to create a concrete version of the concept, the *Begriff.* To do this he must free it from the image, the *Bild*. The *Phenomenology of Spirit* is a grand project to accomplish this separation of the concept from the image. Hegel's philosophy considered as a whole is about the nature of the *Begriff*. Throughout this work I have simply used the term "concept" for Hegel's *Begriff*.

The contrast I make between *Bild* and *Begriff* is not Hegel's. Hegel does not employ *Bild* in the *Phenomenology* as a special term. I have introduced the contrast to refer to the general, systematic problem of the separation between image and concept that I find in the *Phenomenology*. Hegel's own contrast is between *Vorstellung* and *Begriff*. Hegel employs *Vorstellung* in the sense of pictorial or figurative thought, especially in relation to his contrast between religious and philosophical thought. *Vorstellung* in its general usage need not refer to thought involving an image but only to a mental process that is not as such conceptual. I mean *Bild* to refer to all modes of *bildhaftes Denken*—all forms of imaginative thought, religious, aesthetic, and mythical, that is, forms of thought that depend upon the metaphorical power of language. My use of the term *Bild* is most directly suggested by Hegel's description of his work as a *Galerie von Bildern,* a picture gallery, at the end of the *Phenomenology*.

Much of my grasp of the general *Problematik* of the relationship between *Bild* and *Begriff* in philosophical thought I owe to Ernesto Grassi of the University of Munich. Grassi's *Macht des Bildes, Die Macht der Phantasie,* and other works have caused me to see the importance of metaphor and the role of rhetoric in the philosophical enterprise. Our common research and our conversations in Germany, Switzerland, the United States, and at his villa on the island of Ischia in Italy have stretched over nearly ten years and have had an important influence on the shape of this text. I thank Professor Grassi for reading the manuscript of this work and offering valuable criticism.

There are many great commentators on Hegel; one whose writings have had a special effect on my thought is John Findlay. In his work, *Hegel: A Re-examination,* which brought Hegel back into the English-speaking world in our time, Findlay is as sensitive to the power of Hegel's metaphors and ironies as he is to Hegel's deep rationality. In his chapters on the *Phenomenology* Hegel's metaphors live, and Findlay adds to them metaphors of his own. Each time Findlay does this he enriches in a few sentences our vision of Hegel. It was Findlay's work that first suggested to me the approach of this study, much as it in the end differs from Findlay's interpretation of Hegel.

Quentin Lauer, in his presidential address to the 1982 meeting of the Hegel Society of America, took up the theme of "Hegel as Poet" (published in the proceedings, *History and System*, State University of New York Press, 1984). What he said is an invitation to consider Hegel in a new light. Lauer asks: "Did Hegel himself in his speculative philosophizing exercise an art which, although it cannot be included under any of the genres he enumerates, is nevertheless poetic? " The question is, of course, rhetorical, but Lauer makes his intention in raising it quite clear:

> Philosophical language cannot entirely dispense with propositional form—
> but neither can it be tied down by it. One might well ask whether
> philosophical writing that dispenses with a highly imaginative use of
> language is adequately philosophical. One thing, at least, seems abundantly
> clear: it would be an injustice to Hegel to lump all his philosophical
> writing under the heading of *prose*—despite the efforts of so many of his
> commentators to render him prosaic. His own constant insistence both
> that the mere proposition is inadequate to express philosophical truth (he
> was impatient with propositional form—it does not get said what needs
> to be said), and that there is a greater affinity between poetic imagination
> and speculative reason than there is between understanding and reason,
> precisely because poetry is preeminently illustrative of the dialectical
> movement of spirit, make it clear that, whether or not we want to look
> upon Hegel's writing as poetic, we are sure to misread him if we read
> what he writes as prose and only prose.

Further on Lauer says: "The most obviously poetical of Hegel's works is, of course, the *Phenomenology of Spirit,* shot through as it is with poetic imagery, symbol, and metaphor (which may well be the reason why the *Phenomenology* receives such short shrift from prosaic-minded commentators), but imagery, symbol, and metaphor do not stop there." Lauer goes on to suggest that imagery, symbol, and metaphor are necessasry not just for the comprehension of Hegel's text but for the comprehension of Hegel's subject itself—the speculative understanding of history, reality, and spirit. I could not agree more. I do not mean that what I have said in this work is what Lauer intends. His views and mine are different. But his address states what is at issue in the reading of Hegel today.

I wish to thank my students, who heard these lectures in an earlier version in my seminar on the *Phenomenology* during fall term 1980 at The Pennsylvania State University and during fall term 1983 at Emory University, whose combination of scepticism and appreciation has had a beneficial effect on my thinking. I wish also to thank my wife, Molly Black Verene, who has been the first reader of these ideas and has helped greatly to give them life.

D.P.V.

Atlanta

CITATIONS IN TEXT

Quotations from Hegel's *Phenomenology of Spirit* are from A. V. Miller's English translation, occasionally adjusted by my translation. Citations are to the system of paragraph enumeration introduced in Miller's translation. These are often followed by the corresponding page reference in J. Hoffmeister's German edition and in some instances by reference to J. B. Baillie's earlier English translation.

I have employed Miller's translation because it appears at the moment to have become the standard text for English readers of Hegel and because it is more accurate than Baillie's on most passages. But Baillie is more eloquent. Baillie's renderings of Hegel's metaphors and poetical expressions often achieve a higher English and are more forceful and memorable than Miller's.

Phenomenology of Spirit, trans. A. V. Miller with analysis of the text and Foreword by J. N. Findlay. Oxford: Clarendon Press, 1977.

The Phenomenology of Mind, trans. J. B. Baillie, rev. 2d ed. London: George Allen and Unwin, 1949.

Phänomenologie des Geistes, ed. Johannes Hoffmeister, 6th ed. Hamburg: Felix Meiner Verlag, 1952.

One

Introduction: Hegel's Imagination

What is Hegel's *Phänomenologie des Geistes—Phenomenology of Spirit* (1807)? There are two basic answers current among Hegel's readers and commentators. (1) One group sees the *Phenomenology* as an early, adventurous attempt by Hegel to state the nature of his system. These readers see Hegel's metaphysical logic of categories as the true basis of his system, or, more specifically, his logic together with his philosophy of nature and of spirit that make up his *Encyclopaedia of Philosophical Sciences.* The *Phenomenology* is understood as a work peculiar to a period in Hegel's own philosophical development and his understanding of the need to counter the abstract conception of the absolute present in his day. The true aim of Hegel's thought is the presentation of the self-active concept or *Begriff* which is achieved in his *Logic,* that of his larger *Science of Logic* or his shorter version in the *Encyclopaedia.* The *Phenomenology* is a pathway to the metaphysical-categoreal articulation of the concept that is the subject matter of the *Logic.* Once this pathway is followed to the standpoint of mind of the *Logic,* it has fully served its purpose.

In its extreme form the emphasis on the *Logic* and the *Encyclopaedia* as the mature version of Hegel's system becomes a criticism of the *Phenomenology.* In his recent edition of *Hegel's Philosophy of Subjective Spirit* (1978), M. J. Petry says: "Once he had drawn the distinction between Phenomenology proper and the rest of the Philosophy of Spirit, Hegel seems never to have entertained any thought of treating his earlier work as an integral part of the mature system. It was not to be rejected outright, since for all its imperfections it could not be regarded as entirely at odds with systematic thinking, but it was quite obvious that there was no point in encouraging anyone to take it very seriously. In the introduction to the Encyclopaedia, as we have seen, the three ways in which we relate to objectivity are presented as basic to systematic thinking (secs. 26–78), and there was quite evidently no doubt at all in Hegel's mind that he was better employed

1

making use of commonsense realism, empiricism and philosophical principles in working out a satisfactory dialectic of Anthropology, Politics, History, Art, etc., than in phenomenologizing." [1]

(2) The other group of readers and commentators has focused attention on the *Phenomenology* as such, as a work of independent genius. Among these are French interpreters such as Jean Hyppolite and Alexandre Kojève. Such interpreters are impressed with Hegel's connection of forms of consciousness with forms of existence, particularly forms of social existence. The genius of the *Phenomenology* is seen to lie in Hegel's power actually to describe many of the fundamental characteristics of the human condition. This second approach to the *Phenomenology* sees it as a contribution to existential phenomenology and not simply the pathway to the *Begriff* realized in the *Logic*. Richard Kroner, in introductory remarks on Hegel's philosophical development, says: "The *Phenomenology* finds the eternal within the present. By reconciling the extremes of time and eternity, it lets existence and essence coincide and thus gives fresh speculative meaning to the idea of existence. Not Kierkegaard, but his great master, Hegel, was the inaugurator of existential philosophy." [2]

I wish to advance a third approach to interpretation of the *Phenomenology,* one which has no precedent among interpreters of Hegel. It is original. No one, to my knowledge, has suggested it. It allows us to see something about Hegel's work that none of the views of the other two types, or those that might be graded in between, permit. In the introduction to his edition of the *Phenomenology,* Johannes Hoffmeister says the difficulty of this work does not lie in entering into the onset of the work, nor in habituation to its style and the special senses of its concepts, nor in the acquisition of its content, but in carrying on to the end with Hegel's method, following his course of thought to the last page.[3] This is exactly what I wish to do. The last page of the *Phenomenology* is a remarkable one. And it is a page that has gone without extensive comment by Hegel's interpreters, even those who have done a section-by-section commentary.

On this last page, and by this I mean the last paragraph of the work beginning on the penultimate page, in this final moment of his work, Hegel introduces the term *Erinnerung*—"recollection"—which he employs four times in this short space, in one instance italicizing it and hyphenating it as *Er-Innerung*. Hegel employs the term here in a sense quite different from his use of it in other places, where he regards recollection as a particular moment of intelligence in his account of the psychology of theoretical mind (e.g., *Philosophische Propädeutik* (1809/11), secs. 135–44 and *Encyklopädie der philosophischen Wissenchaften im Grundrisse* (1830), secs. 452–60). His senses of recollection in these places, for example, are similar to what Aristotle discusses in his short treatise on memory and remembering in the *Parva naturalia*,[4] that is, senses of recollection that are now well-known. But in the *Phenomenology* Hegel uses *Erinnerung* in a unique sense crucial to his whole philosophy.

On this last page of the *Phenomenology* Hegel uses *Erinnerung* to describe what the phenomenology of spirit is. In other words, Hegel waits until the last page, and in fact the last sentence, to give a name to that power of consciousness by which consciousness can have a speculative knowledge of its own activity. Here Hegel says that the forms of spirit in their contingency are history and in their conceptual organization are the science of the coming into appearance of knowing, and that both together are conceptual history or recollection. *Erinnerung,* which can be translated by the English word "recollection," but which does not preserve the sense of "inner," *das Innere,* is the master key to the *Phenomenology.* Hegel's work is a colossus of systematic memory.

Hegel's regular commentators have given no special attention to Hegel's use and hyphenation of *Er-Innerung.* Ernst Bloch, in a lecture on language and culture, remarks: "In Hegel's *Phenomenology* one notices quite frequently how a sudden linguistic insight is inextricably bound up with true philosophical invention. This occurs when Hegel separates the word re-collection *[Er-Innerung]* and thereby takes recollection (as the condition of history) into the most interior, the most subjectivistic opposition to 'alienation' *['Entäusserung']* (as the condition of nature). Naturally, this inward, self-returning, subjectivistic sense of the word recollection would not have been usable if the concept *[Begriff]* had not been the guiding factor in the matter; but a reciprocal action of the inventions nonetheless exists." [5] The hyphenation is an act of genius on Hegel's part that calls the reader's attention to the fact that *Erinnerung* is the master key for understanding how to read the *Phenomenology* as a special process of the inwardizing of the subject.

What does it mean to claim that the key to Hegel's *Phenomenology* is *Erinnerung?* Simply put, it claims that speculative knowing, *spekulatives Wissen,* presupposes recollection. The *spekulative Satz,* the speculative proposition, that Hegel discussses in the Preface, in which the substance of the judgment passes from subject to predicate, requires powers of mind that are not in themselves logical, nor can they assume logical form. These powers are not anti-logical or illogical or irrational. They are the constant companions of speculative knowing, but, by their very nature, cannot take the form of the speculative proposition. Recollection proceeds through metaphors, ingenuities, and images; it gives us access to the whole gallery of images through which consciousness brings forth its starting points and restarting points in the course of its being. To recollect is not to form a proposition, but to form an image. An image is not a proposition nor is it implicitly a proposition. But an image can give access to the proposition. The *Bild* is the basis of the pathway of the process of consciousness of

the *Phenomenology.* This pathway is its *Bildung.* The *Bild,* the image, is
the form through which *Erinnerung* works.

A glance of the table of contents of Hegel's *Phenomenology* shows how
much it is a *Galerie von Bildern* (gallery of images or picture gallery), as
Hegel calls it in the last paragraph: the *verkehrte Welt* (topsy-turvy world),
Herrschaft und Knechtschaft (masterhood and servitude), the *unglückliche
Bewusstsein* (unhappy consciousness), the *geistige Tierreich* (spiritual animal
kingdom), the *schöne Seele* (beautiful soul), etc. These are not accidental
features of Hegel's text. They make the text itself possible, just as the
images themselves make consciousness itself possible. These are not embellishments of Hegel's dialectic, but actual carriers of his thought. The
view that comes closest to my own on this point is Carl Vaught's in *The
Quest for Wholeness:* "In fact, the frequent occurrence of metaphorical
discourse in the *Phenomenology* gives Hegel's thought its initial richness
and provides him with a linguistic medium in terms of which to make
philosophy concrete." [6]

Once this is understood we are on the edge of being able to enter into
Hegel's course of thought, to recover our own recollective powers of
interpretation and escape the night of logical triplicity that forgets the
dependency of speculative knowing on the image. In what follows I wish
to consider several points that may help make clear some of the implications
of my claim and serve to modify some of the natural resistance to the
originality of its thesis. They concern the meaning of the final passage of
the *Phenomenology,* in more detail than I have yet mentioned, the notion
of *Schein* or appearance, and Hegel's doctrine of *Vorstellung* and *Aufhebung.*

The final full paragraph of the *Phenomenology* is as follows:

> The other side of its [spirit's] becoming, *history,* is *knowing,* self-*mediating*
> becoming—spirit given up into time; but this giving up is precisely the
> giving up of itself; the negative is the negative of itself. This becoming
> presents a languid movement and succession of spirits, a gallery of images
> *[Galerie von Bildern],* each of which, endowed with the total riches of
> spirit, moves so slowly because the self has to penetrate and digest these
> full riches of its substance. Since its completion consists in fully knowing
> what *it is,* its substance, this knowing is its going *into itself* in which it
> abandons its existence and gives its shape over to recollection [1]. In its
> going into itself, it is sunk into the night of its self-consciousness, but its
> vanished existence is preserved in it; and this transformed *[aufgehobene]*
> existence—the foregoing, but out of knowing newly born—is new existence,
> a new world and shape of spirit. Spirit has to begin unbiased from its
> immediacy in this new world and move once more to maturity, as if all
> that preceded was lost and it had learned nothing from the experience of
> the earlier spirits. But the *re-collection* [2] has preserved this and is the
> inner being, and, in fact, higher form of substance. Thus, when this spirit

begins its formation once again anew, appearing only to proceed from itself, it begins at the same time on a higher plane. The realm of spirits which have formed themselves in this way in existence make up a succession in which one takes the place of the other and each has taken possession of the empire of the world from the predecessor. Their goal is the manifestation of depth, and this is the *absolute concept [Begriff]*; this manifestation is the transformation *[Aufheben]* of its depth or its *extension,* the negativity of this I as being in itself, which is its giving up *[Entäusserung]* or substance—and its *time,* so that this giving up itself gives up to itself and in its extension, just as in its depth, is the self. The *goal,* absolute knowing, or spirit knowing itself as spirit has for its path the recollection [3] of spirits as they are to themselves and accomplish the organization of their realm. Their preservation on the side of their free existence, appearing in the form of contingency, is history, but on the side of their conceptually grasped organization is the *science* of *the coming into appearance of knowing;* both together, conceptually grasped history, form the recollection [4] and the Calvary of absolute spirit, the reality, truth, and certainty of its throne, without which it would be lifeless solitude; only—

> from the chalice of this realm of spirits
> foams out to Him, His infinity.[7]

What immediately precedes this final paragraph is spirit as nature. Spirit as the forms of nature is a form of forgetting, of wandering with strange companions, not itself. It saves itself from these strange companions, the objects of nature, by remembering it has another life—a life of self images. It recalls that it has another life free of the mindlessness of natural science, that it is capable of *Bildung.* At the first moment [1] recollection produces history as nightmare, as a procession of scenes such as pass before the self in its own night of individual life. But in the second moment [2] the fact that recollection is itself a systematic power is realized. Recollection is not merely the entertainment of the image but the internalizing of the image. Thus Hegel hyphenates his term as *Er-Innerung. Erinnerung* is a process of *Innerung,* of inwardizing the image. This inwardizing is the basis of *Bildung.*

The third moment [3] is the assertion that this power of recollection to inwardize is what gives access to absolute knowing, *absolutes Wissen,* that it is its prime pathway. It brings forth the actual appearances through which absolute knowing can be reached. The fourth moment [4] is the realization that recollection in both its sides—in its power to call forth images and in its power to *know* them, to organize them into a totality— is conceptualized history, *begriffene Geschichte.* Hegel claims further that this appearance of the concept as recollection is Calvary. The spirit is brought by recollection to its place of the skull, the Golgotha, the place of crucifixion.[8] I think Hegel means this image even in a completely visual sense. What seemed to be the face, the living presence of mind or spirit suddenly becomes the *calvaria*—the skull lacking the lower jaw and facial portion. Here once again the image shows us what it is not: the concept as the element of the divine in the image has not attained its proper life.

The *Phenomenology* ends with an image. Hegel quotes his own modification of the last two lines of one of Schiller's earliest poems, "Die Freundschaft" ("Friendship") (1782). Hegel's commentators read right past these lines, ignoring the fact that Hegel closes the *Phenomenology,* not with a concluding discursive statement, but with a poetic-religious image. Schiller's poem is philosophical-cosmological in intent. It explores the love between friends and the dialectical oppositions within the cosmos—earth and sky, matter and spirit, etc. Herbert Cysarz, in his study of Schiller, says that the ideas of the poem "remind one of Herder, Hemsterhuis, Ferguson, Hutcheson, Shaftesbury, especially Leibniz and finally Plotinus." [9] To see Hegel's point, the full last stanza of Schiller's poem must be considered. It is a double portrait of the divine: of divine mastery by its powers to create a spiritual realm, but also of divine failure to create a likeness, a companion. The divine is left with its own infinity as companion. It is thrown back into its own movement.

> Freundlos war der grosse Weltenmeister,
> Fühlte *Mangel*—darum schuf er Geister,
>   Selge Spiegel *seiner* Seligkeit!—
> Fand das höchste Wesen schon kein gleiches,
> Aus dem Kelch des ganzen Seelenreiches
>   Schäumt *ihm*—die Unendlichkeit.

> Friendless was the great World Master,
> Felt a lack—thus he created spirits,
>   Blessed mirror of His bliss!—
> Still found the highest being no likeness
> From out of the chalice of the whole realm of the soul
>   Foams for Him—infinity.[10]

In his quotation of this at the end of the *Phenomenology* Hegel modifies the last two lines of the poem to read: "aus dem Kelche dieses Geisterreiches/schäumt ihm seine Unendlichkeit." Thus he substitutes "dieses Geisterreiches" ("this realm of spirits") for "des ganzen Seelenreiches" ("the whole realm of the soul") in the first line and "seine Unendlichkeit" ("His infinity") for "die Unendlichkeit" ("infinity") in the second line.

The infinity that Schiller leaves us with suggests what Hegel in the *Science of Logic* calls the "bad infinite" *(Schlecht-Unendliche),* the infinite that just goes on and on. By transposing the line to "His" *(seine)* infinity,

Hegel suggests the "true infinite" *(wahrhaft Unendliche),* the infinite of
an existing whole that systematically and determinately recapitulates itself.[11]
What is recapitulated is the *Geisterreich,* the realm of spirit in all of its
various moments and stages that is presented in the *Phenomenology of Spirit.*
At the end of Schiller's poem the World Master or God is left in pathos.
The divine fails to create a companion equal to himself. In Schiller's version
pathos prevails because God's existence is left in the condition of the bad
infinite. In Hegel's version God's existence has a tragic face. God's relation
to the forms of His creation is that of fellow sufferer. Although his being
is that of the true infinite, he suffers the quest to make actual and determinate
all the moments within His infinite.

In Hegel's version the World Master is left with the re-collection of his
own creation as, in fact, are we, the readers. We are given a final image
in which to recollect the pathway we have travelled. We must recall the
forms of spirit that are really ourselves—our infinity. The first language
of infinity is the image; infinity can later be formed as a concept. Hegel
ends his whole work with an image, an image of the inability of the divine
to bring its own creation and its own being to a point of rest. We, the
readers, like the divine, are forced back into the forms of our creation to
produce the perfect friendship that makes their truth the whole.

Concerning the sense in which the end is the beginning Quentin Lauer
says: "Once more we see how this final chapter of Hegel's *Phenomenology
of Spirit* serves as an 'introduction' to a second reading. Spirit returns to
the 'immediate' beginning to grow once more from there, as though it had
missed the point of all the successive stages in its progress. When it does
so, however, it finds that 'memory [*Er-innerung* = 'interiorization'] has
retained them and is the inner, which is in fact the higher, form of
substance'." [12]

I can now explain my title of this chapter—why it is Hegel's Imagination
rather than Hegel's Recollection. The image is the form of recollection.
It is the object *inwardized.* It is consciousness taken into itself so that
substance becomes subject or the self as appearance itself. Further light
can be shed on this inwardizing accomplished by recollection by Hegel's
lecture manuscript for the *Realphilosophie* of 1805/06, just prior to the
publication, in 1807, of the *Phenomenology.* Here much of the passion and
feeling of the *Phenomenology* is present in these fragmented sentences, even
though Hegel is speaking of recollection as a part of purely subjective spirit
in a section that corresponds with what was to become the discussion of
intelligence in the *Philosophy of Spirit.*

> The human being is this night, this empty nothing, that contains
> everything in its simplicity—an unending wealth of many presentations,
> images, of which none happens to occur to him—or which are not present.
> This night, the inner of nature, that exists here—pure self—in phantas-

magorical presentations, is night all around it, here shoots a bloody head—
there another white shape, suddenly here before it, and just so disappears.
One catches sight of this night when one looks human beings in the eye—
into a night, that becomes awful, it suspends the night of the world here
in an opposition.

   In this night being has returned. . . .

*   *   *

   Recollection adds the moment of being for itself—I have already once
seen it (for my own being superficially conjoined to the perception), or
heard; I recollect; I see, hear, not merely the object, but go thereby within
me—recollect myself, I withdraw myself from the mere image, and place
myself in myself; I place myself especially to the object.

   This being for myself, that I place before the object, is that night, that
self wherein I sunk the self, the now shown forth, is the object itself to
me—and what is before me is the synthesis of both, content and I. . . .

*   *   *

   This (Inwardness, the self that is there) that I the thing only as sign,
but its essence as I, as meaning, as reflection perceived in itself, is just
so object itself; it is immediate innerness first, it must enter also into
existence, object becoming, opposite this innerness to be external; return
to being. This is language as name-giving power, (Memory, creative power)—
imagination given only empty form, signifying [power] of form as internal
placing, but language [placed internality] as individual being. . . .

*   *   *

   Through the name the object as individual being is born out of the
I. This is the first creative power, that spirit exerts; Adam gave all things
a name, this is the sovereign prerogative and first taking possession of the
whole of nature or the creation of this out of spirit; *logos* reason essence
of the thing and speech, fact and fable, category. Man speaks to the thing
as his, (and lives in a spiritual nature, in his world) and this is the being
of the object. . . .

   The world, nature is no more a realm of images, inwardly transformed,
that have no being, but a realm of names. That realm of images is the
dreaming spirit, that has to do with a content, that [has] no reality, no
existence—its awakening is the realm of names; here separation is at the
same time, the dreaming spirit is as consciousness; only now its images
have truth. . . .[13]

Recollection gives us being for itself and the image that becomes the name.
By the power of the name the world is transformed into a world for spirit.

In his well-known letter to Voss of May 1805, written near the time of this lecture manuscript, Hegel said: "Luther made the *Bible,* you have made Homer speak German—the greatest gift that can be made to a people . . . so I wish to say of my own endeavor, that I wish to attempt to teach philosophy to speak German." [14] The *Phenomenology of Spirit* is a recollection, an *Er-Innerung,* of the deepest meanings of language and the German language. [15] The *Phenomenology of Spirit* is the entrance of philosophy into language and, since all language is a particular language, it is the entrance of it into German. Hegel's task is much different than either than of Luther or Voss, who are translating meanings from one language to another. Hegel must through the power of recollection bring forth and make visible speculative knowing. Recollection engenders speculation. But speculation will fall into lifeless solitude the moment it loses its friendship with recollection. To form the words of natural language into philosophical language, into concrete concepts, is to replicate on a higher level the transformation of images into names in the invention of language itself.

The first use of the expression, *Phänomenologie,* as a part of a philosophical system is in the work of the eighteenth-century mathematician, scientist, and philosopher, Johann Heinrich Lambert—*Neues Organon oder Gedanken über die Erforschung und Bezeichnung des Wahren und dessen Unterscheidung von Irrtum und Schein* (New organon or thoughts on the investigation and indication of truth and the distinction between error and appearance) (1764). The general intent of Lambert's work is a reform of Wolffian logic. It concludes with a theory of appearance, of *Schein,* in which Lambert uses the title: *Phänomenologie oder Lehre von dem Schein.* Lambert calls his *Phänomenologie* a "transzendente Optik." [16] This "optics" allows us to see through forms of appearance, avoid error, and employ human reason. On September 2, 1770, Kant wrote to Lambert: "A quite special, though purely negative science, general phenomenology *(phaenomenologia generalis),* seems to be presupposed by metaphysics. In it the principles of sensibility, their validity and their limitations, would be determined, so that these principles could not be confusedly applied to objects of pure reason, as has heretofore almost always happened." [17] In his letter to Marcus Herz, February 21, 1772, Kant wrote that he planned to write such a general phenomenology, as the first part of a metaphysics. [18]

How does Hegel come to write the *Phenomenology of Spirit?* Beginning in the Winter Semester 1801/02 Hegel delivered a lecture course on logic and metaphysics. From this point on Hegel is involved in the attempt to develop a system of speculative philosophy organized on the three-part plan of the later *Encyclopaedia,* of logic and metaphysics, philosophy of nature, and philosophy of spirit. He develops this in his teaching. In the Summer Semester 1806, in a course on speculative philosophy, Hegel lectured for the first time on phenomenology and logic. Hegel probably began writing his manuscript in the spring of 1806. In his course announcement for Winter Semester 1806/07 *Phenomenology* is used for the first time. A Phenomenology of Spirit is to be given as an introduction to Logic and Metaphysics. This was apparently Hegel's concept of the book he was preparing, but the Phenomenology grew under his hands and became the work itself, which was finished in October and published in April of the following year—1807. In between October and January Hegel wrote the Preface.

I mention these well-known facts to suggest that Hegel, like the Enlightenment minds of Lambert and Kant before him, conceived phenomenology to be a brief negative science that would clear the way for an account of truth or the principles of truth. The result was different. Once undertaken systematically the doctrine of *Schein* consumed the whole of Hegel's original attempt at speculative philosophy. *Schein* is a labyrinth, an *Irrgarten,* "garden of error," in which a sense of the unseen must always be present in order to find its pathway.

Schein, "apparency," stands between *das Wahre,* the true, and *Irrtum,* error. Its meaning is close to its literal meaning of *shining forth.* It is the seen. Hegel's problem is to take the fundamental distinction of metaphysics between the *seen* and the *unseen* and find it as the basic principle of the "seen," of "apparency." This apparency, *Schein,* becomes *Erscheinung,* "appearance, phenomenon"—a totality, a world of the seen. This totality is not the true or real, *das Wahre,* but what is *wahrscheinlich, Wahrscheinlichkeit,* probability, likelihood.

In apparency the seen shines forth. The form of apparency is the image, the *Bild,* not the concept, the *Begriff.* But the *Begriff* shines forth from the *Bild.* I can only keep my head about me within the world of the seen by a grasp of the unseen. To have this grasp of the unseen I see it as phenomenon. My sense of the unseen always takes me immediately beyond the given seen such that it appears to me as phenomenon. *Erinnerung* forms apparency as *Erscheinung* through the *Bild,* through the night of its gallery of images. The movement, the dialectic of the unseen against the seen is my pathway, my travel *(fahren)* through the *Erscheinung.* In other words it is *Erfahrung* (experience). *Erinnerung* is the producer of the *Bild* which points to the *Begriff,* the unseen element that is the basis of speculative knowing. Recollection is the constant companion of speculation as the image is the ever-present key to the concrete concept. These come about through the sense of the opposition of the seen and the unseen that takes consciousness on its voyage of discovery, its *Erfahrung.* This is what happens when consciousness steps between the true and error. When this step is taken abstract conceptual thinking is left behind and recollection, the "memory-image," as a way of knowing is discovered. This is what Hegel discovered when he lingered so long in this middle ground. It is a kind of transcendent optics in which the unseen is always the transcendent perspective systematically in the seen.

In my view the dialectic of Hegel's *Phenomenology* becomes a kind of ingenuity *(ingenium)* to move the recollection in the direction of the speculative apprehension. The dialectic is not a method. Hegel is clear on this—that it is no method in any known or ordinary sense. The dialectic is not a method but a name for ingenuity, ingenious activity itself, which takes a continually varying shape depending on the content before it. The problem with which consciousness is always struggling is the limitation of the image, the production of the unseen. Or, put another way, it is driven toward the *sight* of the unseen—the transcendent optics of a situation. The speculative element is there in the determination of consciousness not to be overcome in any given moment by the shining forth, the apparency caught up in the image. The dialectic is the wiliness of the moment required to be beyond the image, to produce the speculative sense of the unseen. This happens first when the image is transformed into the name. The power of the name is the first glimmer of absolute knowing and this power is seen from the first moment of the *Phenomenology* with the attempt to make here, now, and this into names.

To approach the meaning of the *Phenomenology* through recollection and the image, *Erinnerung* and *Bild,* requires some remark on Hegel's views of *Vorstellung* and *Aufhebung,* two of his most famous terms. Is not the interpretation I propose subject to Hegel's criticism of *Vorstellung?* Hegel separates the thought of *Vorstellung,* usually translated as "pictorial thinking," from the thought of absolute knowing, *absolutes Wissen.* Such pictorial thinking does not reveal the true. It does not allow the *Begriff* to confront and manifest itself in its own true form. Because of its involvement with the image, the thought of *Vorstellung* that we find in art and religion falls short of truly speculative thought. This is generally taken to mean that all involvement with the image is pursuit of a false absolute. The image must be left behind when we pass on to the thought of the concrete metaphysical category. The ladder of the *Phenomenology* is to be thrown over at the door to the *Logic.*

I claim this to be incorrect and a limited grasp of the Hegelian enterprise. It depends on a commitment to the either/or in thought that Hegel's sense of thought is against. Central to the dialectic of Hegel is *Aufhebung.* As is well known, this word is not translatable into English. We do not have this perception in the mentality of the English language.

The verb *aufheben* has four senses in English: (1) to lift or raise something up (as in the simple sense of *heben,* to raise); (2) to take something up, to pick it up, or even seize it actively; (3) to keep or preserve something, to retain it; and (4) to abolish, annul, cancel, to put an end to something. Hegel uses the term *aufheben* and its noun *Aufhebung* in all four senses at once: the sense of actively raising and picking something up so that it is preserved and held on to, yet in this act something of it is lost and annulled. It ceases to be what it was, but yet lives on in a new state. This is what occurs when one stage of consciousness is taken up into a succeeding stage through the negation of the former. The one is *aufgehoben* in the other, exists as a transformed presence in the other. The physical actions of meanings (1) and (2) parallel the more spiritual meanings of (3) and (4) of this very ordinary German verb. To raise something up is a way of keeping or holding to something but to pick something up carries a sense of selection in which something is taken from its context and thus some of what it was in its context is cancelled and annulled.

The relationship between absolute knowing and those forms of spirit that lie just below absolute knowing is one of *Aufhebung.* The thought of *Vorstellung* must be *aufgehoben* in absolute knowing, *absolutes Wissen.* The image of *Vorstellung* that is perhaps best translated as presentation, but is also sometimes translated as imagination, must be there in absolute knowing in a transformed sense. *Vorstellung* has the sense of that which has been placed before, what has been *vorgestellt.* It has the sense of that which has been perceived being placed in a manner ready for cognition. It is placed before cognition in a mode of formation adequate to the properties of what is perceived. It also has the sense of what is past being renewed—the perception is presented.

Because it is *aufgehoben,* the thought-world of the images of *Vorstellung* present in religion and art has an effect and a definite presence in the thought-world of absolute knowing. Recollection is the necessary access to speculation. Speculative knowing can never make itself out of itself, but has its presentational moment. The image, the *Bild* (as that which is *vorgestellt* in *absolutes Wissen* through the general process of *Erinnerung*) must be capable of being found in the *Begriff.* The presentational image is always the basis of the life of the speculative proposition. They are the friendship of thought.

In conclusion let me state some of my points. These are intended as leads for investigation, not as presently established interpretations.

(1) The view I am suggesting is possible only if one notices something about Hegel's *Phenomenology;* namely, that Hegel's table of contents is set in terms of metaphors and images and that much of the book itself turns about these. Further, one must notice that these are not simply examples or embellishments or tricks that Hegel has inserted into his thought. They are an integrated part of it. The *Phenomenology* moves through them and they constitute the most memorable part of the work, e.g., the mastery and servitude metaphor.

(2) This presence of metaphor and image fits with Hegel's own final placement of his project in recollection.

(3) The dialectic, that Hegel says is a method that is not a method, is a process within recollection. It is thus not a logic or protologic. Hegel's dialectic is a way of structuring ingenuity (Latin: *ingenium*).

(4) *Begriff* is always in connection with *Bild.* Recollection is the basis of speculation. It gives speculation its necesary beginning points. Any given stage of consciousness must have its preceding stage within itself. It must contain its own immediate origin as well as the origin of consciousness itself. There is thus a recollective moment forever within absolute knowing because of Hegel's sense of *das Aufgehobene.* When we look properly within the *Begriff* we find there the *Bild,* the product of *Erinnerung.* The *Begriff* is no monotone of itself, its own metaphysical categories in sequence. It is forever in friendly opposition to the image—its own origin, present in itself.

Two

The Method of In-itself

Hegel's introduction to the *Phenomenology* has no specific title. Traditionally it is said to state the "intention and method of the present work." [1] This is to say that it is an introduction—a place where we are given in a few pages some general elements of the work. It is right to focus on method, because the theme of the introduction is method. Hegel's presentation of this theme follows an ancient principle that he does not state: to say what a thing is, say what it is not and say what it is. In the first eight paragraphs Hegel says what method is not (Miller, 73–80); in the following nine paragraphs Hegel says what method is (Miller, 81–89).

According to this principle, when one has said what a thing is not and what it is, one has said all there is to say about a thing. Hegel begins by saying what method *seems* to be and ends by saying what it *is*. The crucial distinction for all thought between what seems and what is the case determines the style of Hegel's introduction. In the introduction Hegel has said all that there is to say about the method apart from its presence in his subject matter, a point that he suggests in the first sentence: "It is a natural assumption that in philosophy, before we start to deal with its proper subject-matter, viz. the actual cognition of what truly is, one must first of all come to an understanding about cognition, which is regarded either as the instrument to get hold of the Absolute, or as the medium through which one discovers it" (Miller, 73).

I wish to focus my remarks on these last nine paragraphs where Hegel says directly what his method is, going back into the first part of the introduction at points where it throws light on the second part. The central idea of Hegel's general description of method in the *Phenomenology* is the *Ansich,* the *in-itself.* The conception of the *Ansich* is the point around which Hegel's description of method revolves. When we grasp the role of the *Ansich* in consciousness we will be able to see how Hegel proposes to treat the distinction he makes in the first sentence of the introduction between

14

cognition *(Erkennen)* and the absolute *(das Absolute)*. The *Ansich* is the middle term whereby Hegel can set in motion the distinction between the absolute as something beyond cognition and cognition as the act of knowing that requires an object more specific than the absolute for its activity.

Knowing that has only the contrast between (a) the absolute as a maximum and (b) specific cognition cannot pass beyond the principle of noncontradiction. Such knowing must always function in terms of one object in opposition to another. Hegel's conception of the *Ansich* allows him to have a conception of the absolute that has a positive, rather than a merely negative connection with cognition. The absolute is something other than a merely negative limit for cognition. This requires a sense of that which is *ansich* as not merely a limit for cognitive activity.

I wish to organize my remarks around three points: (1) how the conception of *Ansich* works as the basis of Hegel's conception of method; (2) how this conception of method might be related to the notion of ingenuity (Latin: *ingenium)* and why it is helpful to introduce this word to understand Hegel's conception of method; and (3) how Hegel's conception of method can be projected in relation to the style of the *Phenomenology* with its reliance on images or *Bilder* for crucial turning points in the progression of consciousness.

(1) The way in which Hegel describes the method of the *Phenomenology* is best described as a two-step movement or a movement of two moments. If we attempt to characterize it as a movement of three moments, as readers of the *Encyclopaedia* might wish to do, we lose sight of the distinction Hegel is concerned to develop between the *Ansich* and the *Ansich* known. And, if we try to proceed to a third moment, we find we must go further, to even a fourth moment. We are then thrust back on the method as two moments that produces a further version of itself—a second pair of moments. At this point we have no third moment but twos at every juncture: an original set, a second set, and a twoness of the two sets themselves. This is, I am aware, an original way to read the introduction and Hegel's method therein. I invite you to read it with me.

There are two passages in which Hegel states, with complete directness, the points upon which his phenomenological method rests. He says: "But the distinction between the in-itself and knowledge is already present in the very fact that consciousness knows an object at all. Something is *for it* the *in-itself;* and knowledge, or the being of the object for consciousness, is, *for it,* another moment. Upon this distinction, which is present as a fact, the examination rests" (Miller, 85). So that there can be no mistaking Hegel's clarity here, the final sentence of this quotation is, in the original text: "Auf dieser Unterscheidung, welche vorhanden ist, beruht die Prüfung" (Hoffmeister, p. 72). This is Hegel's fundamental discovery: that there are two moments of consciousness, neither of which can be in any sense or manner reduced to the other. Neither is the ground of the other. These are two senses of the in-itself, the *Ansich,* that each requires the other. There is, to put it simply (1) a consciousness of something (something that is not a product of consciousness is there in itself before consciousness), and (2) a consciousness that this something is an object for consciousness (a consciousness of the consciousness of the object).

If the reader of Hegel's work does not grasp personally, in himself, the sense of difference between these two moments, the basis of Hegel's thought will be forever closed to him. There is one point I wish to stress about the connection between these two moments, namely, *that it is not a relation.* Consciousness of the object as an *Ansich* and consciousness that this object as *Ansich* is an object for consciousness is not a relation. It is not a *Verhältnis;* it is not a *Beziehung;* it is not a *Zusammenhang,* although with this notion of "hanging together" we come closer to the meaning. These two moments of consciousness are that which makes the notion of relationship possible. They are the sine qua non for relation itself. Relations or categories—that which holds something together as a single—are expressions on the level of thought of this primordial power of consciousness to produce for itself these two self-requiring moments. The *Ansich* is not there as object for consciousness unless it knows it to be there and it can only attain this realization if it has already grasped it. This is what Hegel means by *experience (Erfahrung),* and by his work being a "science of the experience of consciousness" (see below, Appendix).

The mutual, self-requiring nature of the two moments of consciousness is what Hegel means by necessity. What we can ever mean by necessity in experience is this sense of the self-requirement of these two moments. One is not possible without the other. Necessity is not a relation. But any kind of relation we would wish to speak of in the progression of the stages of experience in the *Phenomenology* is an attempt to formulate in a single idea the meaning of the bond that actually exists between these two moments of consciousness *in* and consciousness *for* itself. Every shape consciousness gives to itself attempts to express the absolute gap that exists between these two moments as one particular relationship or another. But the gap as such is just necessity. Consciousness cannot induce from its first moment its second, nor can it deduce from its second moment the first moment. They are themselves the bond of necessity that makes experience possible for consciousness.

Experience is this *doubled Ansich.* Without it there is no such thing as experience, human experience. Consciousness *travels* within itself *(fahren, erfahren)* in terms of the unevenness of these two moments. For this unevenness Hegel uses the term *dialektische Bewegung,* dialectical movement in the introduction. What this means is that consciousness is unable to hold these two *Ansich*s before it àt once. It is either feeling the object or feeling itself out of the object, as having apprehended the object. Consciousness seeks to have these two moments that are the basis of its experience become *entsprechend*. Hegel says: "But the *goal* is as necessarily fixed for knowing as the serial progression; it is the point where knowing no longer needs to go beyond itself, where knowing finds itself, where concept corresponds to object and object to concept" (Miller, 80—revised to read knowing for *Wissen* and concept for *Begriff*). To be clear: the end of the sentence reads, "der Begriff dem Gegenstande, der Gegenstand dem Begriffe entspricht" (Hoffmeister, p. 69). The goal, the *Ziel*, of knowing consciousness is the state wherein concept and object *sich entsprechen*.

To describe this Hegel uses the verb *entsprechen*. This has the sense of answering, suiting, matching, being in accord with, meeting with, corresponding. Hegel does *not* say that this highest state of knowing, absolute knowing, is based on a *unification*, on a unifying of the concept and object. These two elements attain a new answering, an accord. The term *entsprechen* preserves the notion of speaking, *sprechen*, and adds the prefix *ent-*. This prefix as such designates the entering into a new state or the abandonment of an old state, if we consider it purely in philological terms. These two, the object and the concept, attain a co-responding. In the last sentence of the introduction Hegel says that consciousness will arrive at a point where "die Erscheinung dem Wesen gleich wird," where the appearance and essence become *gleich*. He does not say they become *identical*, but *gleich*— the same, like, equal, equivalent, alike, similar, resembling, proportionate. He does not say that they become identical, become one, merge into a unity, manifest a common principle, or exist through a common element. They reach a stage in which they are the same, alike, proportionate.

How many falsehoods about Hegel have been told by failure of attention to this point, a point that Hegel makes clear from the start, in his introduction? Who has turned into questions what Hegel means by such terms as *entsprechen* and *gleich*, the terms he uses to describe how the concept and the object stand to each other at the level of absolute knowing? The answer is: no one. His commentators fail to stay awake at this point.

Hegel points out that when through scepticism we discover an untrue mode of knowing, we must further see that our scepticism is itself a position that results from this negation. The second passage on which I want to remark specifically is this: "It shows up here like this: since what first appeared as the object sinks for consciousness to the level of its way of knowing it, and since the in-itself becomes a *being-for-consciousness* of the in-itself, the latter is now the new object. Herewith a new pattern of consciousness comes on the scene as well, for which the essence is something different from what it was at the preceding stage. It is this fact that guides the entire series of the patterns of consciousness in their necessary sequence" (Miller, 87).

The last sentence of this passage is like the last statement of the earlier quotation concerning the distinction upon which the examination rests. Hegel goes on to connect the notion of necessity to the origination of this new object: "Nur diese Notwendigkeit selbst, oder die *Entstehung* des neuen Gegenstandes . . ." (Hoffmeister, p. 74). The distinction between the two *Ansich*s allows us further to understand what necessity is, what a necessary connection is. A necessity is the inability of one thing not to accompany another. Thus, in the grasp of the two levels of *Ansich*—consciousness of the object and consciousness of the object for consciousness—the root meaning of necessity is grasped. The motion of this second sense of the *Ansich* entails further that it become a being-for-consciousness: "das *Ansich* zu einem Für-das-*Bewusstsein-Sein des Ansich wird.*" Note that this new object is not described by Hegel as a synthesis of the original two senses of the *Ansich*. He does not call this new object even an in-and-for-itself, an *An- und für sich Sein*. He calls it a "Für-das-Bewusstsein-Sein des Ansich"—a "a for consciousness being of the in-itself." This in-itself is not a synthesis but a new return to immediacy, a new birth of the object, a new origination, an *Entstehung,* a new standing. This new standing is also an old standing, a reaffirmation of the primordial status of the *Ansich*.

The *Ansich* comes again, working in from around consciousness's back, as Hegel says. This is no mere repeat of the original *Ansich,* for it is the result of it. But if this new object is a third moment, then we can expect a fourth moment when consciousness, by the necessity present in the first two, moves back from this new object and sees it, too, as an object that it knows. It should now be clear that every move consciousness makes is a reaffirmation of the original two moments of the *Ansich*. What consciousness seeks to discover, to realize is these two moments as *entsprechend,* as answering to each other in accord, as *gleich,* as alike, proportionate. This will allow it to champion the necessity of its being, to attain the friendship of both its sides of object and concept, to recall the metaphor from Schiller's poem with which Hegel ends the *Phenomenology* itself.

Before moving to my second and third points, I wish to say a word about the "Hegel Legend of 'Thesis-Antithesis-Synthesis'," as it has been called by Gustav Mueller.[2] Mueller thinks that this description of Hegel's dialectical method has arisen because of the difficulties of Hegel's terms themselves. He says: "These linguistic troubles, in turn, have given rise to legends which are like perverse and magic spectacles—once you wear them, the text simply vanishes." [3] Glockner's *Lexikon* shows that Hegel never uses these terms to describe his own philosophy. Hegel's friend, Rosenkranz, author of the first serious book on Hegel, never uses them. As Mueller notes, and George Kline, in an article on Hegel literature in various languages notes also, modern scholarship has made little or no use of this terminology.[4] Only readers of W. T. Stace continue to wear the spectacles.[5] It is perhaps significant that Stace's exposition of Hegel's philosophy is an exposition of the *Encyclopaedia,* which has a triadically structured table of contents.

How did this legend begin, if not from Hegel himself? Mueller discovered that in the winter of 1835–36, about four years after Hegel's death, a group of Kantians in Dresden asked Heinrich Mortiz Chalybäus, a professor of philosophy at Kiel, to lecture on the new philosophy after Kant. They wanted the new philosophy to be a confirmation of their own Kantianism. Chalybäus's lectures, which were published as a book a year later and circulated in three editions, characterized Hegel's method in terms of thesis-antithesis-synthesis, projecting this triplicity on to the trilogy of being, nothing, and becoming that begins Hegel's *Logic*. It is not to the point to pursue Mueller's thesis further here. This triadic reading of Hegel has Kantian origins. In the preface to the *Phenomenology* (Miller, 50), one of only two places where Hegel speaks of triadic thought or *Triplizität,* he identifies it with the abstract formalism of Kantian thinking. In the other place, his lectures on the *History of Philosophy,* Hegel mentions this triplicity of Kant and calls it a *geistloses Schema.*[6]

This touches on a great problem of how to understand the dialectical method in Hegel's corpus as a whole, which I will not pursue further here. How is the twofold description of the method in the *Phenomenology* to be understood in relation to the threefold arrangement and often actual presentation of the contents of Hegel's *Encyclopaedia* and *Logic?* Is this method of the two moments of the *Ansich* the method of consciousness in which the *Begriff* is in active relation to the *Bild?* And is the threefold sense of motion that of thought in which the *Begriff* is the sole occupant of its own realm? The full answers to these questions involve the relationship between the *Phenomenology* and the *Logic.* I have attempted in the Epilogue to suggest where I stand on the general problem of the relation of these two parts in Hegel's system.

(2) I wish now to turn to the connection I suggested between Hegel's conception of method in the *Phenomenology* and ingenuity. The question is this: How are we to understand a method that is not the application of thought to an object? Our sense of method in modern philosophy is set by Descartes' *Discours de la méthode.* Here is the notion of thought as instrument, as *Werkzeug.* Thought can discover the truth about a matter by applying to it Descartes' fourfold method of Part 2 of the *Discours.* Hegel denies the name science to such a conception of method. Such a method cannot secure its own starting point. It presupposes, as in fact Descartes says it must, a first step in which something is recognized as certainly and evidently true. The starting point has no security from scepticism. It must presuppose the overcoming of doubt in order to apply the method to the object under investigation.

Scepticism is the ability to make the certain and evident, uncertain and inevident—to move truth into appearance. Hegel understands that the answer to scepticism is to move within appearance and to generate an absolute standpoint of knowing by causing scepticism to turn constantly in upon the conditions of its own negation of knowledge of the object. In what I have called the first half of the introduction, Hegel remarks on his conception of *determinate negation* as the answer to scepticism (Miller, 79). When a truth about the object is negated by adducing a ground of doubt, the standpoint from which the doubt is formed becomes a further object of examination on which to place new doubt. In this manner consciousness passes through a complete series of illusions, each time seeing the untruth of the object and then the untruth of the perspective from which it saw the object's untruth. Within illusion there is a necessary moment that is based on the double sense of the *Ansich* that Hegel explains in the second half of the introduction.

This is in fact Hegel's notion of *aufheben*—the sense in which consciousness "raises itself on" by cancelling an apparency. This is a methodless method in the sense that consciousness applies itself to itself. Further, because it is self-altering, it is a method unlike any sense of method that can be derived from any other area of thought. In the process of *aufheben,* each moment of *aufheben,* which means each time consciousness passes through the necessity of the double *Ansich,* is different from any other moment of *aufheben.* Method in the ordinary sense requires that the same procedure is constantly applied throughout any alteration in the object. In this case the method alters in itself and in the object. Hegel's sense of method cannot be compared to any sense of method that we know from either before his time or after it. It is not like the hermeneutical or phenomenological senses of method that command so much attention today. Hegel has already rejected these in the first pages of his introduction, as external methods.

My suggestion is that what Hegel calls method is in fact the basis of method, in a sense similar to the fact that what he calls experience is actually the basis of what we more ordinarily call experience. Ingenuity or *ingenium* is not a method in a Cartesian sense but it is a way in which thought accomplishes what it needs to accomplish in any given moment. In its literal meaning it is a natural disposition, a mental power, that which is born in one, a nature, talent. The Latin term has the sense of the perception of the relationships between things which can issue on the one hand in tropic formulations such as metaphor and on the other in scientific hypotheses. *Ingenium* connotes at once the power both to form imagistically and to form through an intellectual principle. It contains both a sense of imagistic and conceptual forming. Through ingenuity a new and needed object is produced through a reshaping of what is already at hand.

In other words ingenuity is a way of doing something that gets its method immediately from the content before it. Each time it makes up its method immediately. It is always doing something for which there is no method. Yet each time such a thing is done it is grasped as a result of ingenuity. Hegel's method of the double *Ansich* is like this. Consciousness must take itself beyond the object to the new object. It must see through the present phenomenon, the seen, to the unseen, to a sense of truth that is beyond the present illusion. Simply on the basis of its present state it must take itself to a further state, one that has never been for it before. It must do this by moving the opposition within the present state somehow against itself until the new sense of the object emerges. As it engages in this production of states of itself it holds its past lines of production in its memory, its recollection. Thus its basis for the ingenious production of a next state becomes ever richer in possibilities. This movement is always governed by the double sense of the *Ansich,* the necessity within conscious-ness itself. The answer to scepticism is this sense of ingenuity. Scepticism that, as Hegel says, just throws things into the same empty abyss (Miller, 79) is simply a failure of ingenuity while at the same time claiming it is ingenuity itself. What sceptic does not think himself the most ingenious of men?

I have introduced the notion of ingenuity to find terms through which we can speak about Hegel's sense of a method that is not like any other method. I have done this in an effort to interpret Hegel in more than a repetition of his own words, a practice which so many writers on Hegel adopt. So much interpretation of Hegel will not dare anything; it engages in a kind of deft furniture moving—lifting a heavy chunk of *Begriff* here and placing a shackly *Gegenstand* there. Having made the connection with ingenuity, we can now say, not that ingenuity has told us what Hegel's method is, but that Hegel's sense of method has told us what ingenuity is as a philosophical power of mind.

Allow me to recast my point and state it again. The great question with the *Phenomenology* and with Hegel's philosophy in general is: What is the dialectic? The dialectic of the *Logic* may be different from that of the *Phenomenology,* but my view at the moment is confined to the *Phenomenology.* To answer the question of what the dialectic is by laying out as a scheme the stages of the *Phenomenology* (or in fact any part of Hegel's system) is a mistake, as it offers us only the table-of-contents mentality of the Un-derstanding and does not allow us (in fact may produce a barrier) to apprehend the self-movement of reason. We create a skeleton of spirit with tickets stuck all over it and learn nothing. The stages of the *Phenomenology* are definitely progressive but at many points it is a mystery how progress from one stage to another is made. The logical mind—that oriented toward argument and deduction—focuses on those stages where the *Aufhebung* seems most proficient and the progression most evident. It then tries to explain those places where the dialectic seems simply to jump to a new stage. What if we approach the movement within the *Phenomenology* in the reverse, and see the jumps as the common state of affairs and the moments of smooth transformation as the exceptional? On my reading, the dialectic is fundamentally a series of fascinating jumps.

What consciousness needs at the end of a stage, when it exhausts itself, when its sense of reality on that stage begins to fall in upon itself, is to grasp a new connection between things. Spirit requires an ingenious act, in which through an immediate act of its own wit it produces a new standpoint. It requires the power of *ingenium*. What is accomplished through *ingenium* is a new *similitudo,* a new likeness, resemblance, a new simile. Spirit must suddenly project a new reality for itself out of a reality in which it finds itself becoming exhausted and dismembered.

Spirit can do this only by attention to the negative, to the fact that it has come to a point where it is in despair. Hegel says: "Spirit is this power only by looking the negative in the face, and tarrying with it. This tarrying with the negative is the magical power that converts it into being" (Preface, Miller, 32). What is this magical power *(Zauberkraft)?* It is the power to form a new *similitudo.* This tarrying *(Verweilen)* with the negative is *ingenium.* When thought is blocked, it requires a new connection with itself. The forging of a new connection does not take place as a simple act of novelty. The dialectical move forward requires *Erinnerung.* Spirit must recollect something from its past state in order to get beyond its present negative state to a new form of itself. The *similitudo* it requires is between what it is at this present moment and what it was, what it can recollect of itself. It requires a simile that will offer it an image of itself that will allow it to convert itself into being. *Ingenium* in Hegel's terms is a movement from *being-in-itself (Ansichsein)* to the *recollected in-itself (das erinnerte Ansich)* that is "ready for conversion into the form of *being-for-self [Fürsichsein]* " (Preface, Miller, 29).

Hegel uses the tropes of metaphor and irony to characterize various stages in the *Phenomenology* and as a weapon to attack opposing positions and states of mind. The whole table of contents looked at from this perspective is a table of metaphors. In saying this I do not mean that all headings employ metaphors. They do not. A look at the contents makes this clear (see below, Appendix). But remember Hegel's "gallery of images." Hegel uses irony to exclude other positions. It is his principal weapon, for example, when he speaks against other doctrines of the absolute ("the night in which all cows are black"), or against phrenologists, or against ethical views ("the law of the heart and the frenzy of self-conceit"). He makes them into jokes.

The trope puts one word in place of another. The metaphor or *translatio* makes use of one word instead of another that is more literal. The irony does this too, because it replaces the "proper" word with an exact opposite. Irony transfers or turns meaning over to its opposite. To the logical mind, the Understanding in Hegel's terms, tropes are improper forms of speech because they are imprecise. Logic attempts to exclude all such figurative meanings. But from the standpoint of dialectic and Reason, tropes allow thought to enter into new stages of consciousness. Tropes are not arbitrary because the *translatio* presupposes the discovery of a *similitudo* that makes the transfer possible. The introduction of the metaphor or irony always gives consciousness a new lease on life.

Another way to put what I am saying is this. Hegel's critique of deduction or mathematical method in the Preface to the *Phenomenology* is well-known to any reader of the work (Miller, 42–47). In the deductive proposition the subject and predicate remain separated. Form remains separate from content. Opposed to this formulation of thought is the "speculative proposition" *(spekulativer Satz)*, the form of the proposition appropriate to dialectical thought (Miller, 61). In this proposition the subject is extended into the predicate and the meaning of the predicate must ultimately be found by returning from it into the subject term.

In traditional discussions of this point it is shown that the deductive proposition that is formulated by the Understanding is really a form of interrupted or internally broken-up dialectical thought. R. G. Collingwood has shown this with great skill in his "logic of the overlap of classes." [7] The relationships internal to the speculative proposition are more fundamental than those of the proposition formulated by the Understanding. The relationships between subject and predicate of ordinary class logic can be derived simply by assuming the exclusivity of the subject and predicate classes. The copula then becomes only a link between two separate classes.

But if deductive thought really presupposes dialectical thought on what does dialectic depend? My point is that dialectic is really a logical way of describing what are essentially rhetorical processes or rhetorical powers of the mind. Their form is essentially tropic and this form is evident in the metaphors and ironies through which Hegel has spirit or *Geist* move. These elements are not accidental but required because of the powers of recollection and ingenuity that are present in consciousness itself.

Two elements are ingredient in *Aufhebung* (the act of preserving and cancelling)—*Erinnerung* and *ingenium*. In any moment of consciousness's development *Erinnerung* produces the element of the old (what is preserved) and *ingenium* strikes the new chord, produces the new relationship that cancels the actuality of what was before. But this new chord is not something wholly new; it is a new chord struck within what is held forth in memory. To read the *Phenomenology* the individual consciousness must enact this process within itself as it follows the *Bildung* of consciousness in general. I must *look* (i.e., recollect) and *see* (the ingenious moment). The *Phenomenology* is a passionate work because it is continually causing the reader to draw forth from consciousness, to recall what was and to see a new connection. In this way the ladder that Hegel says the reader has a right to demand (Miller, 26) is built before one's eyes.

To comprehend what dialectic is we must consider what Hegel describes it not to be, but we must at the same time see what he in fact draws on to make dialectic create its "science of the experience of consciousness."

What are present but not discussed are these powers of mind that are classically excluded from discussion in the idealist tradition which suffers from Descartes' and Locke's exclusion of the rhetorical powers of mind from the pursuit of truth.[8] Hegel may be unaware of the rhetorical basis of his work and only somewhat aware of the extent to which he uses metaphor and irony. He is certainly aware in that he, like other great philosophers, employs them. But he has no reflective interest in the meaning of such devices. Hegel's interest is in the *Begriff*, but the road past ordinary logical meanings to this higher sense of the concrete concept is the metaphor which always points to what is not present in the logical sense of things.

(3) I come now to my final point, which is a remark on how Hegel's notion of method can be projected in relation to his style in the *Phenomenology*. When Hegel is speaking about the new object of consciousness, that which is born out of the awareness that the object is not only something in-itself but has a being for us, he says: "From the present viewpoint, however, the new object shows itself to have come about through a *reversal of consciousness itself*" (Miller, 87). In the original he says: "durch eine Umkehrung des Bewusstseins selbst" (Hoffmeister, p. 74). This new object requires an *Umkehrung,* an overturning, a reversal of consciousness that comes out of consciousness itself. This *Umkehrung* is the crucial moment whereby consciousness produces a progression of its states to pass beyond living in an illusion or in the dead nothingness of scepticism. It is the turning that consciousness requires in order to achieve a further state of its own being.

How can such a turning, such a reversal of state be accomplished? Let me say it very simply. The metaphor. What consciousness requires to have the new object is a new *arche,* a new first principle. *Archai* come from nowhere. They come when needed and they come from nowhere. They are drawn forth from consciousness suddenly and without method, that is, without some set procedure.[9] Consciousness turns to itself and suddenly has in its hands something of itself that it did not know was there in any explicit sense. This drawing forth of *archai* is like recollecting. It is in fact recollecting in its primordial sense. It is *Erinnerung.* The speech of *archai* is always non-propositional speech. It is the speech of an opening up that allows us to see but not truly to think. It is *bildhaft* but it is not *begrifflich.* It is a kind of speech in which consciousness opens itself to itself.

The metaphor always shows us something from which consciousness can then withdraw and attempt to understand what is seen. The speech whereby consciousness has a beginning point never is derived from anything—it simply appears. If consciousness does not die in a present moment, cease to have experience, it (the new standpoint) appears at the necessary time. We are now in a position to see why the metaphor is a part of Hegel's *Phenomenology.* It is in fact part of his method. The fact that Hegel suddenly presents us with new beginning points of consciousness that do not seem to follow from the state of consciousness before them is not an incomplete element in his account but the basis of the account itself. Once we understand that his method is built upon the two moments of the *Ansich,* in which one moment simply appears from the other, we see that consciousness's apprehension of the object continually comes from nowhere out of itself.

Because consciousness in its own actual progression comes to its new beginnings through metaphysical speech, the science of the experience of consciousness must have this as an element of its presentation. This speech is there as part of its deliberate recollection of the path of consciousness. For the actually developing consciousness these metaphors of beginning points are reals. For the consciousness that has in some sense reached absolute knowing, these metaphors are keys to the state of consciousness on any given stage of its course. Thus the metaphors or images in the *Phenomenology of Spirit* are not just any metaphors but the metaphors of consciousness itself, those by which it accomplishes the turning, the *Umkehrung,* of its being at any given moment. The *Phenomenology of Spirit* is a philosophical speech in which all the powers of language, its imagistic and its conceptual powers, are brought forth so that the reader may recollect. This recollection is the process of internal vision that all speculation requires. It is the constant companion, the friend, of speculation.

I know how strange it must seem, in an atmosphere of conceptual reasoning, to point to the metaphors that occupy many of the section titles of Hegel's work. Let me point to some words of Hegel that often have been overlooked. These are from what has come to be called "The Earliest System-Program of German Idealism," which is dated by Otto Pöggeler as written by Hegel in 1796 or the first months of 1797, ten years before he wrote the *Phenomenology of Spirit.*[10] Hegel says:

> I am now convinced that the highest act of reason, that in which it embraces all ideas, is an aesthetic act and that *truth and goodness are siblings only in beauty.* The philosopher must possess just as much aesthetic power as the poet. Men without aesthetic sense are our literal-minded philosophers *[unsere Buchstabenphilosophen].* The philosophy of spirit is an aesthetic philosophy. One can in no way be ingenious *[geistreich],* one cannot even argue *[raisonnieren]* about history ingeniously *[geistreich]* without aesthetic sense. Here it ought to become clear what it really is that men lack, who understand no ideas and who frankly enough admit that for them everything is obscure as soon as it goes beyond the table of contents and the index.
>
> Poetry gains a higher dignity, it becomes at the end again what it was at the beginning—the *teacher of humanity;* because there is no philosophy,

no history left, the poetic art *[Dichtkunst]* alone will survive all other sciences and arts. . . .

First of all I shall speak here of an idea which, so far as I know, has never occurred to anyone else—we must have a new mythology, but this mythology must be in the service of ideas, it must be a mythology of *Reason.*[11]

Hegel wrote these words when he was twenty-six.[12] They are not the final words of his system, or are they? In the last book he published, the *Philosophy of Right,* Hegel closes his preface with his most famous words, his most quoted lines—his metaphor of philosophy as the owl of Minerva spreading its wings at dusk. This has practically become the emblem, the seal of his thought. Hegel never loses this sense of image and he makes it the continual entry point of his speech. Hegel continually surrounds himself with the art of the *poeta*—the maker.

Three

Das Meinen, "Meaning"

The title of the first chapter of the *Phenomenology* faces us with three terms which we must come to understand through the medium of sense or the sensible. They are *Gewissheit* or certainty, *das Diese* or this, and *das Meinen* or "meaning." Although this chapter, that in its full title is "Die sinnliche Gewissheit; oder das Diese und das Meinen" ("Sense-certainty; or This and 'Meaning' "), is short, it is one of the eight chapter-divisions of the *Phenomenology*. It is, in fact, the shortest of the eight. Despite the shortness of its length, it carries one-eighth of the conceptual weight of the work, and partly because of limits of length, it attains an eloquence of discussion matched by only a few other moments in Hegel's work.

If both Hegel's conception of *die sinnliche Gewissheit* and *das absolute Wissen* can be in some way grasped, we will have before us the whole circle of Hegel's doctrine of *Schein*. The end point of consciousness and of the science of the experience of consciousness is the absolute form of *Wissen* in which the concept and object correspond *(sich entsprechen)*. This depends upon *Erinnerung*, recollection, and its articulation in philosophical language—the language of the *Phenomenology* itself. The *Phenomenology* portrays consciousness as beginning not with *Wissen*, but with *Gewissheit*, certainty. The first attempt that consciousness makes at self-definition, at agreement of the concept with the object, takes the form of certainty achieved through the powers of sense. The first moment of recollection is sensing. And we learn immediately in this first chapter that sensing is a form of recollecting. Only when consciousness can remember what is happening to it in its moments of sensing, can it get free of its belief that it can achieve certainty in the senses. Consciousness learns in this first form of itself that its attempt to be without *Bild* or *Begriff*, in short without language, and simply to sense the object is not possible. (1) What is the beginning point of consciousness, according to Hegel? And what is the

27

beginning point of our understanding of the beginning of consciousness, the perspective of the *we* of the *Phenomenology* in its first moment of understanding consciousness? These are the first questions I wish to discuss. (2) Then I wish to inquire into the meaning of Hegel's remark on the Eleusinian mysteries.

(1) Hegel describes this first stage of consciousness directly in terms of the twofold sense of *Ansich* that he states in the introduction. Hegel says: ". . . in sense-certainty, pure being at once splits up into what we have called the two 'Thises', one 'This' as 'I', and the other 'This' as object" (Miller, 92). Hegel's description of the two senses of *Ansich* in the introduction is completely general, as two moments present in any stage of consciousness—the object as immediately present in consciousness and the object as something for consciousness. Here, in the first stage of consciousness in its movement toward absolute knowing, the *Ansich* appears as *This*. Pure being, This, appears as a double This—This as object and This as I. Further, consciousness at the stage of sense-certainty believes a certain relationship to hold between these two moments. Hegel says: "One of the terms is posited in sense-certainty in the form of a simple, immediate being, or as the essence, the *object;* the other, however, is posited as what is unessential and mediated, something which in sense-certainty is not *in itself* but through [the mediation of] an other, the 'I', a *knowing* which knows the object only because the *object* is, while the knowing may either be or not be" (Miller, 93).

Sense-certainty attempts to overcome the equal claim that each of the two moments the *Ansich* has to being by asserting the reality of the first over the second. Thus the *knowing* or 'I' is held as inessential and dependent on the object as if the object could be there without the knowing I. We as the onlookers in this process know from the introduction that both moments are necessary in order that consciousness have experience *(Erfahrung),* that experience means just the movement begun through the tension of this primordial split. Throughout this stage of sense-certainty consciousness struggles to hold on to this affirmation of the object, only to assert the essentiality of the *I,* in the very last sentence of the chapter, in an effort to escape the difficulties of confining being to the This. Consciousness does this by claiming the This of the I as essential. It claims that what is there depends upon consciousness taking up in itself what is there as truth. What is crucial is that I *"perceive* it" *(nehme ich wahr).*

In the chapter on sense-certainty Hegel also includes a version of what he calls the "new object" in the introduction. In the introduction Hegel says that the object "sinks for consciousness to the level of its way of knowing it, and since the in-itself becomes a *being-for-consciousness* of the in-itself, the latter is now the new object" (Miller, 87). The new object comes about because the being-for-consciousness now simply is, but its *Ansich* is not identical as the original first moment. In the middle of the chapter on sense-certainty, when consciousness has become frustrated in its efforts to write down on paper its attempts at the immediacy of here and now, Hegel considers whether this immediacy can be achieved by the act of pointing-out, by an *Aufzeigen.* We can attempt an ostensive definition of its being.

Hegel claims: (1) I point out the now as something that has been; (2) I assert the truth that it has been; and (3) "But what has been, *is not;* I set aside the second truth, its *having been,* its supersession, and thereby negate the negation of the 'Now', and thus return to the first assertion, that the *'Now' is*" (Miller, 107). Hegel numbers these three moments. Notice that the third moment is not called by Hegel a synthesis of the first two. He just says that I "return to the first assertion that the *'Now' is.*" As we follow this paragraph we see that Hegel does not mean that we return to the first moment as such. We do not go back and again point out. The *Aufzeigen* has led us to the Now as universal. But the Now is once again for consciousness. It is once again for consciousness a new object, a new *Ansich*—a universal which consciousness will set about to perceive.

Consciousness gets to this new object, this new grasp of the *Ansich,* not by sensing, but by the primordial form of recollection that is present in the structure of the double *Ansich.* In the second moment, when the object becomes something for consciousness, the first object is recollected in the most primitive sense possible. There is always an *Er-Innerung* of the object in the second moment of the *Ansich.* Consciousness is always more than what is before it. But it must struggle to remember this fact. It is also forever dissolving itself into the object. Hegel says that natural consciousness *(natürliches Bewusstsein)* is always learning from experience what is true in it; "but equally it is always forgetting it and starting the movement all over again" ("aber vergisst es nur ebenso immer wieder und fängt die Bewegung von vorne an") (Miller, 109; Hoffmeister, p. 86). When we (we who can philosophize and are observing sense-certainty) *forget* the history of consciousness that we see here in the *Phenomenology,* we lose our way and think we can achieve truth directly at this level. This recollection of the history of consciousness in its primordial struggles is the basis of proper philosophizing.

I wish to turn now to the theme of "reversal" that runs through sense-certainty. On the last page of this chapter Hegel says: "But if I want to help out language—which has the divine nature of directly reversing the meaning of what is said, of making it into something else, and thus not letting what is meant *get into words* at all . . ." (Miller, 110). In the original this reads: "Will ich aber dem Sprechen, welches die göttliche Natur hat, die Meinung unmittelbar zu verkehren, zu etwas anderem zu machen und so sie gar nicht *zum Worte kommen* zu lassen . . ." (Hoffmeister, p. 89). Language has the "divine nature" of "die Meinung unmittelbar zu verkehren"—immediately to turn meaning upside down. Hegel does not say here that meaning is turned back upon itself *(umkehren)*. He does not speak of reversal in a usual sense, but in a rather radical sense—*verkehren,* to turn the wrong way, turn upside down, turn topsy-turvy, invert. The divine nature of language is to turn things to their opposite. In passing I will note that this use of *verkehren* in the concluding sentence of this first stage of consciousness foreshadows his conception of the so-called "inverted world," the *verkehrte Welt,* with which Hegel concludes the whole (A.) Consciousness section of the *Phenomenology.*

We see in this first chapter that consciousness is born upside down. It comes into its first stage by a reversal to its opposite. How does Hegel do this? He presents this through a *Wortspiel,* a pun, on the term *das Meinen.* This is not a simple pun but an irony. Language catches consciousness in its power to create double meaning willfully. The sense of this fundamental pun cannot be translated directly into English because it depends upon the fact that to be of the opinion of, to mean in the sense of having an opinion, *to opine—meinen* in German—is close to the possessive adjective and possessive pronoun of the first person in German—*mein. Das Meinen* is *mein.* Hegel's irony here is also involved in the sense that what is asserted as objective meaning or *Meinen* to be in the now and the here is really only a meaning as it is in the I as knowing, as *mein.* Hegel is also punning on *mein* as the old genitive singular of *ich* and on *das Mein* in the sense of possession, my own property—*das Mein und Dein,* what is mine and thine. Hegel is playing with the irony of consciousness attempting what it cannot possess, what slips through its hands—the sense-particular. Consciousness becomes so involved in trying to express the meaning of particulars and thus possess a particular that we see it misses even the wisdom of animals.

The *Phenomenology* begins with a joke, with a piece of humor that is philosophically developed. Hegel knows what Shaftesbury made the theme of his great treatise, "*Sensus Communis:* An Essay on the Freedom of Wit and Humour" (1709)—that humor is the means for seriously dispelling illusion.[1] Hegel shows that consciousness in its attempt to possess the real or being in its purity is caught in the irony of language and is thus opened to itself. Language has this divine nature. Hegel uses that same power of the trope of irony to open us, the observers of consciousness, to the folly of sense-certainty. Hegel develops his point of how consciousness exists in the stage of sense-certainty in terms of his dialectical method of reasoning and description, but he lays open his methodological account to us through his play on words of *das Meinen.* The use of this pun, which is not a logical but a tropical device, is the insight upon which the chapter rests. The pun opens up the logical description of the stage of sense-certainty for us. Without grasping this sense of the pun we are at hazard of having to return to the doctrine of truth as sense-certainty and learn again from language itself the irony of this belief.

Of the fourfold arrangement of tropes in modern thought (e.g., that deriving from Gerard Jan Voss), irony is the fourth trope, metaphor is the first (metonymy and synecdoche, the second and third—attribute for thing meant, genus for species or vice versa).[2] Irony is a trope close to dialectic in that the intended meaning is the opposite of that expressed by the words used. Hegel's sense of irony here is not only of this type but is further of the type expressed in the French *ironie du sort* (an irony of fate), in which consciousness experiences a contradictory outcome of events as if to mock the events it could have rightly expected, or would seem it could have expected. Consciousness learns the ironic truth that what is there clearly before it—the particularity of here and now and itself as knowing I— cannot be joined into that which is the very form of itself—its power of language. It could have expected better than to have its sense of being as pure particular turned into the universal through the one power unique to it—its divine gift of language. In simply being itself, its world is turned upside down.

Does the *Phenomenology* start where consciousness itself starts? Or does the point at which we find consciousness derive from other more primordial stances to the object that have taken place before the opening of sense-certainty? Hegel's most powerful critic on this point is the twentieth-century philosopher Ernst Cassirer. In the second volume of *The Philosophy of Symbolic Forms,* which contains his theory of mythical thought, Cassirer refers to Hegel's passage on the ladder in the *Phenomenology.* This is the passage in the preface in which Hegel says that science should provide the individual with a ladder to show him the way to the concept (Hoffmeister, p. 25). Cassirer says: "If then, in accordance with Hegel's demand, science is to provide the natural consciousness with a ladder leading to itself, it must first set this ladder a step lower."[3]

By a step lower Cassirer means that Hegel begins his account of consciousness with epistemologically neutral heres, nows, and I's. In the stage of sense-certainty the object is simply being sensed as a neutral content, neutral as to its primordial feeling qualities. As Cassirer shows in his theory of mythical *Dasein,* the object is first sensed not as a content but as a force. The object is felt in primitive consciousness as a friendly or foreboding presence. Usener, in his classic study of *Götternamen,* a work that was important for Cassirer, sees the first use of language by which consciousness frees itself from the immediacy of the moment of pure being as involving "momentary gods" *(Augenblicksgötter).*[4] Immediacy is first formed not as a this but as a god, a god of the moment. The first use of the name is a mimetic forming of the being of the god in language. Hegel realizes something of this primordial use of the word or name as *Bild* in his lecture manuscript of 1805/06 of the *Realphilosophie.* In his discussion of the origination of the name from the power of *Erinnerung,* he says "Blitz, Donner, Ähnlichkeit mit der sinnlichen Erscheinung."[5] He knows that the

name gives *Geist* access to the object. To consider the name as mimetic
of the sensible object, as in the sound of thunder and the sound of the
word *Donner,* is to have a sense of language the primordial moment of
which is not ironic.

Cassirer's point is that sensory consciousness itself is a dialectical development from an expressive or purely mythic stage of consciousness. On
this level language functions in accordance with the first trope—metaphor—
and is incapable of the reflectivity necessary for the fourth trope, irony.
Cassirer's criticism is a strong and penetrating one, backed up by a full
theory of mythical *Dasein* itself. Hegel sets out to present a doctrine of
appearance that Lambert and Kant saw as a necessary negative science to
open the way to metaphysical truth. Hegel's powerful solution is to allow
consciousness to derive systematically this necessary absolute standpoint
from the motion of consciousness itself. But Hegel's beginning is like that
of every other modern epistemology in the respect that it starts from a
primitive version of common sense, of *gesunder Menschenverstand.* Hegel
fails to see how the mythic-expressive object makes possible the sensory-
perceptive object.

Hegel seems to have grasped myth only as associated with the aesthetic
culture of ancient Greece and with the religions of ancient peoples. Hegel
certainly knew work written directly on myth. Herder and Goethe had
affirmed the importance of myth for the understanding of humanity and
culture. Hegel's own thought was developing during a period of intense
early Romantic interest in myth that began about 1797 in the works of
Friedrich and August Schlegel, Hölderlin, Novalis, and Schelling.[6] Hegel
never saw what Cassirer points to, that myths contain a primordial form
of the relation of consciousness to its object. He never really grasped that
myths were the earliest productions of consciousness, the first language
through which the world was sensed.[7]

This is not to take away from Hegel any of his own sense of the mythic
or metaphorical as an element in philosophical understanding and philosophical speech such as he expresses in the *Systemprogramm* of 1796. I
want at this point to turn to this element in the chapter on sense-certainty,
which was my second original point of concern. But as a final reflection
on the above question, one might say that Hegel must have considered the
mythic origins of consciousness itself and rejected it deliberately as the
origin point of the *Phenomenology.* If so, one might hold that the *Phenomenology* begins when consciousness has its first glimmer of the philosophical
standpoint of mind, when it first very very dimly feels the question of the
true. Against this interpretation would be Hegel's famous assertion that
"the True is the whole." The whole would seem to include mythical
thought. Myth itself is the original artisan of the thought of the whole.
One might expect the science of the experience of consciousness to include
mythical consciousness in its whole, and philosophy, as the thought of the

whole, to take its own origins back to this original artisan. The fact is that most readers of the *Phenomenology* do not ask why sense-certainty is the first stage of consciousness, but just begin with Hegel.

(2) My second point concerns Hegel's image of the "most elementary school of wisdom, viz. the ancient Eleusinian Mysteries of Ceres and Bacchus" (Miller, 109). Those who assert the reality of sense objects in an external world have not learned the lesson of the ancient rites, of the secret meaning of the eating of bread and drinking of wine. Hegel says even animals know such wisdom. Animals do not stand stock-still before sensuous things as if they possessed intrinsic being, they fall to and eat them up. Hegel concludes: "And all Nature, like the animals, celebrates these open Mysteries which teach the truth about sensuous things" (Miller, 109).

Suddenly, near the end of the chapter, after he has spoken of houses and trees, of this noon and this night, of the acts of writing down and pointing-out, and he has set these ordinary acts in terms of the epistemological patterns they involve, Hegel says he will say what is really wrong here: the consciousness of sense-certainty has not learned the wisdom of Ceres and Bacchus. What does Hegel mean by this powerful metaphor? It is powerful not only in itself, as an image set against the blank mentality of sense-certainty, but it is powerful because it refers to the oldest of Western mythico-religious experience. The cult of Eleusis, along with other cults of the mystical revival of the sixth century, had its roots in pre-Homeric religious experience. This image has a resonance with the oldest mentality and ritual activity of the Western tradition.

So that we have in mind what it is Hegel is citing, consider several comments on these mysteries from William Chase Green's classic study, *Moira.* "The Eleusinian mysteries, the ancient fertility rites of the Attic village of Eleusis, held at the time of the autumn sowing, and symbolizing or seeking to assist the rebirth of the dead plant-world each year, were transformed into a ritual that symbolized the hope of human immortality. . . . No moral qualifications were required of the Eleusinian initiate; and the ethical potentialities of the cult were lower than were those of Orphism. Nor did the initiate receive any secret dogma; his craving for immortality received no intellectual confirmation, but rather imaginative support; at the most, he felt a comforting sense of having entered into the experience of a goddess, who might therefore feel sympathy with him." [8] One finds this cult, of course, in the *Bacchae* of Euripides, with its portrayal of Dionysiac frenzy.

This metaphor at the end of sense-certainty is a reflection of Hegel's famous sentence in the Preface: "The true is the bacchanalian revel at which not a member is sober, and because each member no sooner detaches himself than he collapses straightway, the revel is just as much transparent and unbroken calm" (Miller, 47, Ballie, p. 105, Hoffmeister, p. 39).[9] The whole *Phenomenology* is tied to this metaphor. The true is the bacchanalian revel in which the secrets of the eating of bread and drinking of wine are learned. If we cannot enter into these secrets we cannot grasp the true— the doctrine of the experience of consciousness. Even animals have this wisdom of eating and drinking. If we are bad at the rituals of eating and drinking of the bodily digestion of the world, we will be bad at the spiritual digestion of its contents. The secrets at the Dionysiac frenzy were not logical propositions. These were not reading groups that met for the study of the works of Willard van Orman Quine or Saul Kripke. Even most of Hegel's own commentators would have stayed home from such rituals and sought a more sober relationship to the gods. Although Hegelian commentators, unlike logicians of the abstract concept, have an interest in the whole, they usually insulate the *Begriff* in their discussions from the primordial and passionate speech of the world.

Hegel's own speech throughout the *Phenomenology* has three features. Hegel often says things three different ways and the chapter on sense-certainty is a model for this mode of philosophical speech. Hegel uses (1) what may be called rational description. He speaks directly in terms of the method of his philosophy. This is a kind of metaphysical and epistemological language that uses terms like in-and-for-itself, absolute knowing, the *I*, determinate negation, concept, etc. Although many of these terms are used broadly in German speech, they carry special meanings for his thought. (2) Hegel speaks commonsensically. He formulates statements of what he means from ordinary life and speech. This is a language of examples. In the chapter on sense-certainty instances of this are his experiments with noon and night and the tree and the house, elements of common-sense consciousness. (3) Hegel speaks in tropic language, in metaphors and ironies. Here he uses poetic-mythical images. Sometimes these are images of great impact and at other times they are more self-limited, simple poetic expressions.

Considered from another standpoint these three modes of Hegel's philosophical language represent two uses of symbolism to achieve philosophical meaning. The first is that of (1) and (2). It is discursive speech—the use of principles and examples. Hegel explains through the principles of his philosophy a point at issue and offers a common example or illustration of it. The second (3) is a language of images of symbolic statements that are presentational in character. They are neither principles of anything nor examples of anything. This kind of speech is not referential in its meaning but solely presentational. It means just what it says. Its meaning is not in a referential relation back to the rationalistic mode of speech. It extends and deepens our grasp of the philosophical point. Only when both forms of speech are interwoven can we understand in a Hegelian manner. But we have so little experience in taking metaphorical speech seriously as a carrier of philosophical meaning that we read right past it. Hegel does not write past it; but we have become so accustomed to the monotone hum of the abstract concept and the category, the fluorescent buzz of the argument, that we have lost track of the dimensions of philosophical language. We have forgotten its secrets and cannot recollect its manner of eating bread and drinking wine.

The Eleusinian mysteries are connected to the story told in the Hymn to Demeter. Hegel uses the Roman names, Ceres and Bacchus, for Demeter and Dionysus (the Greek goddess of agriculture, especially grain, and the Greek god of wine). Demeter's daughter, Persephone, was carried off by Hades. Demeter roamed the world in search of her, wandering in disguise among men until she reached Eleusis, where she was discovered to be a goddess. She offered to teach the people her secrets of the reproductive powers of nature. Through Zeus's intervention with Hades, Demeter was reunited with Persephone. Because Persephone had eaten a seed of the pomegranate, a sacred food of the underworld, she was obliged to spend one-third of the year in the underworld and the rest with Zeus and the gods of Olympus. Thus during the autumn season on earth the seeds sleep in the ground while Persephone is under the world.

Demeter, who could make the earth barren or fruitful and who had created in her anger a drought upon the world, then taught her secrets of agriculture to Eleusis. "To the Kings of Eleusis, of whom Triptolemus was one, she showed her rites and 'awful mysteries which no one may in any way transgress or pry into or utter, for deep awe of the gods checks the voice. Happy is he among men on earth who has seen these mysteries; but to him who is uninitiated, and who has no part in them, such good things do not befall once he is dead, down in the darkness and gloom.' " [10]

These very schematic remarks on the Hymn to Demeter are enough to suggest what Hegel is calling up as an image from the origins of Western consciousness. Unless we learn the secret of the reversal of the object that makes it nothing that is present in the "divine nature" of language, we are doomed to be forever returning to the barren plain of sense-certainty as the ground of knowing being. Hegel says we continually forget the process of experience and then "fängt die Bewegung von vorne an" (Hoffmeister, p. 86). We then start the movement over again. Hegel brings forth this myth of renewal and production at the beginning of the development of consciousness. He says these are open mysteries of nature. Nature knows the secrets of producing, reducing to nothing what it can produce, and reproducing—the secret known to Demeter. There is no way, no method, that we can learn this process for consciousness except to allow consciousness to move in terms of its own nature, between its own two senses—that of object and object for itself. This turning upside-down that is necessary for the reduction to nothing of what is before consciousness is present in its power of language. Language is the medium of consciousness.

Do I make too much of this metaphor of the Eleusinian Mysteries of Hegel? The image of them was certainly of personal importance to him. In August 1796 he wrote his poem *Eleusis,* the same year as the *Systemprogramm* in which he spoke against the literal-minded philosophers *(unsere Buchstabenphilosophen),* men without aesthetic sense. He called poetry the "teacher of mankind" *(Lehrerin der Menschheit)* and spoke of a need for "a new mythology." Hegel tried to put into the poem the truth as he thought the Greeks had grasped it, as it could be felt and imagined. His draft of the poem includes the lines: "Fancy brings the eternal nigh to sense,/and marries it with form." [11] As H. S. Harris says, at this point in Hegel's development *"Phantasie* must give place to *Vernunft."* [12]

In the *Phenomenology of Spirit, Phantasie* still gives place to *Vernunft,* but *Phantasie* is not replaced by *Vernunft.* Hegel no longer holds the same view of poetry and poetic making, of *Dichtkunst,* that he does ten years earlier in the *Systemprogramm,* but anyone who reads the *Phenomenology* can see that he has not forgotten it either. The *Dichtkunst* is still there, still bringing the eternal into sense and marrying it to the form of the *Bild* in order that the act of recollection can take place. The point of this recollection is the *Begriff.* This is the goal of the *Phenomenology.*

Hegel's commitment to art and to mythology in this period is not limited to the *Systemprogramm.* In a fragment called "Über Mythologie, Volksgeist und Kunst" (On mythology, "national spirit," and art) recently discovered in manuscript in Berlin, Hegel identifies art with Mnemosyne (Memory) whom he calls the "absolute Muse *(die absolute Muse)."* [13] In this little-known manuscript on the Staatsbibliothek Preussischer Kulturbesitz in Berlin, Hegel says:

> Mnemosyne, or the absolute Muse, art, assumes the aspect of presenting the externally perceivable, seeable, and hearable forms of spirit. This Muse is the generally expressed consciousness of a people. The work of art of mythology propagates itself in living tradition. As peoples grow in the liberation of their consciousness, so the mythological work of art continuously grows and clarifies and matures. This work of art is a general possession, the work of everyone. Each generation hands it down embellished to the one that follows; each[14] works further toward the liberation of absolute consciousness.
>
> Those who are called geniuses have acquired some special skill or other whereby they make the general forms of a people their work, just as others do other things. What such geniuses produce is not their invention, but the invention of a whole people, or the *finding* that a people has found its essence.[15] What belongs to the artist as such is his formal activity, his particular skill in this kind of presentation and he is brought up to this in the general skill. He is like someone who finds himself among workers who are building a stone arch, the scaffolding of which is invisibly present

as an idea. Each puts on a stone. The artist does the same. It happens to him by chance to be the last; in that he places the last stone, the arch carries itself. By placing the last stone, the artist sees that the whole is one arch; he declares this to be so and thereupon is taken to be the inventor. Or, as in the case of workers who are digging for a spring, he to whom it falls to take up the last layer of earth has the same work as the others. And to him the spring bursts forth.

It is the same with a revolution in a state. We can think of a people as buried under the earth, above which there is a lake. Each intends to be working only for himself and the preservation of the whole by removing a piece of stone from above and employing it in the general subterranean construction. The tension in the air, the general elements begin to change; it produces a desire for water. Uneasy, the people do not know what it is they are lacking and to help they dig even higher in the belief of improving their subterranean condition. The crust becomes transparent. One catches sight of it and calls: "Water!" Tears the last layer away and the lake rushes in and drowns them all by giving them drink. So is the work of art the work of all. There is always one who brings it to its final completion by being the last to work on it and he is the darling of Mnemosyne.

When in our time the living world does not form the work of art within it, the artist must place his imagination in a past world; he must dream a world, but the character of dreaming, of not being alive, of the past, is plainly stamped on his work.

In these views on mythology and art from Hegel's Jena period is an echo of his earlier call for a "mythology of reason" in the *Systemprogramm* and his interest in that same document in connecting philosophy with the life of a people: "until we make ideas aesthetic, that is, mythological, they have no interest for the *people;* and in the reverse until mythology is rational the philosopher must be ashamed of it." [16] Seen from the perspective of these fragments, Hegel is attempting in the *Phenomenology* to connect philosophy with the absolute Muse, Mnemosyne, and to create in the living world of modern culture a philosophy that does not have the character of dreaming. It is a task that art and the mythological cannot accomplish but which can be accomplished when the mythological-aesthetic image is joined with reason. It requires a new sense of Mnemosyne *(Erinnerung)* —the absolute Muse, the Muse of the absolute.

What Hegel is attempting is the labor of Hercules—to overpower the abstract concept of *Verstand* and to produce the concrete concept of *Vernunft.* A crucial moment of this labor is the *Bild.* As Hegel says, the process of the *Phenomenology* involves a *Galerie von Bildern.* We as the observers of the process, as the initiates into the mysteries of the "science of the experience of consciousness," must learn the art of philosophical language as well as the method of the dialectical movement. What Hegel teaches in the *Phenomenology* is a mode of philosophical speech that lets us pass through appearance to the being of the *Begriff*. When we fail to learn this art of speech, then "fängt die Bewegung von vorne an." We speak falsely and our account of the dialectical movement is only the hum of epistemological language claiming to present opposites through the monotone of its own single-speaking medium.

The art of Demeter is the art of bringing the earth to nothing and then reproducing from it everything—the shift from autumn to spring. In thought the secret of this *Verkehren* is in the power of the image which comes forth suddenly from recollection and gives speculation a place from which to bring its sense of the sentence that comprehends through the articulation of its own inner movement.

Four

The Topsy-turvy World

John Findlay says that in the Jena lecture-rooms Hegel was seized by a divine imparting of knowledge: "an afflatus perhaps unique in philosophical history, which affected not only his ideas but his style, and which makes one at times only sure that he is saying something immeasurably profound and important, but not exactly what it is. (I am in this position, despite help, regarding the two intelligible worlds in the section on Force and Understanding.) To comment on Hegel fully would therefore require the same sort of psychological and metapsychological treatment that has long been practised on an essentially rapt man like Shakespeare or on such a Gallic genius as Rimbaud or Mallarmé." [1]

Findlay singles out the section on "Force and Understanding: Appearance and the Supersensible World" as an example of a place in the *Phenomenology* where one feels Hegel is saying something profound, but where one is also unsure of exactly what it is. I agree with Findlay's assessment of this section. I agree further with his sense of Hegel as a rapt man. I would add that unless the ordinary reader of Hegel can attain something of this sense of rapture, Hegel's thought is cut off from him and Hegel remains a kind of skeleton with tickets identifying each part but lacking in divine breath, lacking the afflatus that is truly required for understanding Hegel.

My comments in this chapter are divided into two parts. In the first part I wish to enter this section backwards, by starting with its last moments and then going to some of its earlier moments. I do not intend my comments to constitute a systematic exposition. My intention is only to shed what light I can on a very inspired section of the *Phenomenology*. In the first part of this chapter my comments are organized around two points: (1) the sense in which the *verkehrte Welt* is the founding of self-consciousness and its parallel with the Cartesian *cogito;* (2) Hegel's conception of the *verkehrte Welt* and his use of the syllogism to exposit it.

39

In the second part of this chapter I wish to consider two questions that stand outside the section itself: (1) from where did Hegel derive the term *verkehrte Welt?* and (2) what relationship does this term have to Hegel's fundamental project of creating a system of science *(Wissenschaft)?* Little commentary exists on Hegel's treatment of the *verkehrte Welt.* It is treated interestingly in the commentaries of Hyppolite and Lauer. Kojève, Loewenberg, and Taylor take no interest in it. Findlay makes only a remark in his book (the reason for which is perhaps clarified by his statement quoted above). The topic of the *verkehrte Welt* was opened up by Hans-Georg Gadamer's "Die verkehrte Welt" (1966) and pursued by Joseph C. Flay, "Hegel's 'Inverted World' " (1970). These have been followed by two recent articles (1982) by W. H. Bossart and Robert Zimmerman, and Robert Solomon's recent book, *In the Spirit of Hegel* (1983), has a separate section on the inverted world.[2] The *verkehrte Welt* is, of course, not an individually titled section of the *Phenomenology,* but the image around which Hegel organizes the final comments of his chapter on "Force and Understanding."

I

(1) The thesis of the section on Force and Understanding *(Kraft und Verstand)* is evident in the second part of the title: Appearance and the Supersensible World *(Erscheinung und übersinnliche Welt).* Through the concepts of force and understanding we produce the distinction between appearance and the supersensible world. Broadly put, consciousness has begun with an attempt to secure the external object and the I through the experience of sense-certainty. This has generated an attempt by consciousness not just to sense but to perceive *(wahrnehmen).* In this attempt, in Chapter 2 of the *Phenomenology,* consciousness has apprehended the object as thing and properties. In attempting to grasp the object as thing and properties, consciousness has moved to a more "intellectualist" position, that is, it has advanced from a mere sensing of the object to a kind of thinking of it. In this perceiving of the object it experiences deception because that which holds the object together as properties cannot itself be an object of perception. Hegel says: "as perception, consciousness has arrived at thoughts" (Miller, 132).

The object now becomes a force *(Kraft)* or a play of forces. The object is not perceived, but understood. This understanding *(Verstand)* is a kind of inner force or *Kraft* that allows for the grasp of the object as an outer force or play of forces. Hegel says: "This true essence of Things has now the character of not being immediately for consciousness; on the contrary, consciousness has a mediated relation to the inner being and, as the Understanding, *looks through this middle [Mitte] of the play of Forces into the true background of Things.* The middle *[Mitte]* which unites the two extremes, the Understanding and the inner world, is the developed *being* of Force which, for the Understanding itself, is henceforth only a vanishing" (Miller, 143). The understanding is a power that looks through the *Mitte,* the middle or center, of this play of forces to the background. It sees through to an unseen element. From this power of understanding that allows us to go behind what is there in perception is produced the opposition between the appearance and the supersensible world. This twofold sense of force gives us a twofold sense of experience of the world.

I do not mean these remarks to summarize Hegel's account, but to bring enough of it to mind that we can raise the question: What is the purpose of this discussion of force and understanding? It is to bring about self-consciousness out of consciousness. How does self-consciousness come into being out of this opposition between appearance and the supersensible world? The I is of no interest for consciousness here. Consciousness must undergo an experience that makes it bring forth the I as a force different from understanding—different from a force that brings to consciousness the background of the play of forces of the object. It must bring its being forth as more than a limit, as having its own sphere of power as a self. This happens through the experience of the topsy-turvy or "inverted" world, the *verkehrte Welt.*

The understanding, drunk with its power, produces the conception of the reverse world. It forms the thought that there could be a world the reverse of the one it has secured by its distinction between appearance and reality or super-sensible world. In this thought it grasps that everything it has designated as appearance might just as well be the real and everything that it has designated the real might just as well be appearance. What I see before me may in reality be exactly opposite to what I see. The fact that I can articulate in consciousness the difference between appearance and non-appearance, that I can grasp these as two realms, destroys all possibility of certainty of sense and throws certainty back onto the I that makes the distinction. Through the absurdity of this twoness that goes nowhere, the self as something in itself is born.

What we have here has a striking similarity to the end of the first Meditation in Descartes' *Meditationes de prima philosophia.* Hegel does not himself make this comparison, but it is too obvious not to consider as throwing light on the nature of the *verkehrte Welt.* In the first Meditation Descartes adduces grounds to shake our confidence in sense knowledge and he comes to the conclusion that there are certain truths of thinking that cannot be doubted. This leads him to adduce an ultimate ground of doubt: "I will therefore suppose that, not a true God, who is very good and who is the supreme source of truth, but a certain evil spirit, not less clever and deceitful than powerful, has bent all his efforts to deceiving me. I will suppose that the sky, the air, the earth, colors, shapes, sounds, and all other objective things that we see are nothing but illusions and dreams that he has used to trick my credulity." [3]

Hegel says: "According, then, to the law of this inverted world, what is *like* in the first world is *unlike* to itself, and what is *unlike* in the first world is equally *unlike to itself,* or it becomes *like* itself. Expressed in determinate moments, this means that what in the law of the first world is sweet, in this inverted in-itself is sour, what in the former is black is, in the other, white" (Miller, 158).

When Descartes forms this thought he nearly goes into a swoon. He recovers sufficiently in the second Meditation to propose the possibility of an Archimedean point for thought. He compares his famous assertion of the *cogito* to Archimedes' search for the immovable fulcrum with which to raise the earth from its orbit. Descartes achieves the assertion of the *cogito* as first truth through the hypothesis of the "evil spirit," the so-called *malin génie* (Latin text: " . . . sed genium aliquem malignum . . . "; French text: " . . . mais vn certain mauuais genie . . . ").[4] Descartes' topic is certainty of thought. He moves through doubt of the certainty of the senses to an ultimate doubt of the hypothesis of the *malin génie.* From this he produces a new certainty, that of the "self-consciousness" of the *cogito.*

There are dissimilarities in this movement and Hegel's presentation of the *verkehrte Welt.* Descartes speaks of the evil genius in terms of his notion of abstract negation. This reverse God simply makes untrue what I hold on to as true. The *cogito* or I of Descartes is not the same as the sense of self-consciousness with which Hegel begins the next chapter of the *Phenomenology,* following his discussion of force and understanding. Descartes presents this transition from certainty of sense to evil genius to *cogito* as a piece of deliberate philosophical reasoning. But what is interesting here is just the sense of the *malin génie* itself over and against the *verkehrte Welt.*

The *malin génie* is the colossal thought that the world as understood and perceived is precisely illusion, that things are absolutely other than we experience them. This thought gives Descartes the place to stand to lift the world. The *cogito* principle is the lever. Hegel, in his *Lectures on the History of Philosophy,* says: "René Descartes is in fact the true beginner of modern philosophy, insofar as it makes thought from the principle." [5] Hegel calls Descartes a hero. He says: "He began from the first, from thought as such; and this is an absolute beginning." [6] Hegel emphasizes that Descartes began modern philosophy by his shift of the center of philosophical thought to the side of the subject. It should be pointed out that Descartes' conception of thought is not that of Hegel. It lacks Hegel's understanding of the internal movement of thought. But it should also be remembered that for Descartes *cogitatio* is a wider idea than the English term "thought." The certainty of the *cogito* is present on the basis of various modes of mental activity (see the definition of thought in the second Meditation).

Joseph Flay, in his article "Hegel's 'Inverted World'," has interpreted this section of the *Phenomenology* by connecting it to Kant's distinction between phenomena and noumena, remarking that "if Kant had pursued the argument further, the history of German idealism would have been different." [7] Kant in his theory of the understanding *(Verstand)* failed to carry out to its natural conclusion the distinction between appearance and the supersensible. I would add that Kant's failure to carry through to the consequences of such a distinction of two worlds must rest on his decision to abandon the writing of a *"Phänomenologie überhaupt,"* about which he wrote Lambert.[8] I find Flay's connection of this section with Kant helpful. In connecting this section with another thinker Flay joins (as he notes) Hyppolite, who connects it to Christian doctrine, and Gadamer, who connects it to Plato and Aristotle.[9] I also agree with Bossart that: "The difficulty here is that suggestive as they may be, such references do not go to the heart of Hegel's meaning in these passages, for the positions which he is analyzing are so abstract that they cannot be identified with any historical position." [10]

I wish to add Descartes to this list because of the parallel this suggests between the origin of modern philosophy itself and the shift between consciousness and self-consciousness in the dialectical development of natural consciousness. Gadamer has hinted at this in his essay, "Die verkehrte Welt." [11] Historically Descartes begins modern thought with his discovery of the certitude of the *I think*. The crucial moment in this discovery is the grasp of the "evil genius"—the possibility of a cosmic deceiver who is the exact opposite of God. In the Christian doctrine God is the supersensible who provides the certainty to thought that, although some things in the world are illusions, the world itself, the world of appearance, is not defective. The thought that there could be a reverse God, an evil genius or spirit, makes possible the new certainty of the *I think*. Hegel says that when the inner world becomes the supersensible beyond it stands off against appearance as the completely empty, "which," Hegel says, "is even called the *holy of holies*" ("welches auch das *Heilige* genannt wird") (Miller, 146, Hoffmeister, p. 112). When this supersensible becomes more than a limit and has content, it need not be a force that makes the contents of appearance true, but that makes them exactly false.

(2) I wish now to turn directly to the concept of the *verkehrte Welt* itself, to the notion of the experience of world-reversal. In Descartes' undeveloped notion of the *malin génie* we see that in order for thought to make itself a basis of itself, it must raise the question of the total falsity of the object as it appears. In Hegel's concept of the *verkehrte Welt* we see that in order for consciousness to make itself a basis of itself, it must experience the reversal of its own power over the object. The deception,

the *Täuschung,* that consciousness first experienced in its attempt to grasp the truth of the object through its perception has now become systematic deception. It becomes a trauma that shakes consciousness completely. Here the deception involves a sense of self-deception.

Hegel presents the *verkehrte Welt* in three ways, exploiting all the basic powers of language available to him. (a) He presents it directly in conceptual terms; (b) he offers common-sensical examples; (c) he holds the presentation together with a poetic image of the upside-down world.

Hegel first describes the *verkehrte Welt* as a feature of the dialectical movement of consciousness. He says, for example, that this tranquil kingdom of laws that is the copy and support of the perceived world is transformed into its opposite. This happens because: "The *selfsame* really repels itself from itself, and what is not selfsame really posits *[setzt sich]* itself as selfsame. In point of fact, it is only when thus determined that the difference is *inner* difference, or the difference *in its own self,* the like being unlike itself, and the unlike, like itself. *This second supersensible world* is in this way the *inverted* world and, moreover, since one aspect is already present in the first supersensible world, the inversion of the first" (Miller, 157). Here Hegel is saying in discursive terms, the terms of his conception of consciousness, how the "tranquil kingdom of laws" *(das ruhige Reich der Gesetze)* passes to its opposite.

Hegel follows this by a series of examples of what is meant by this logical description. He says in this inverted world the south pole is the north pole and the reverse. The oxygen and the hydrogen poles of electricity are reversed. What is crime in one world is to be honored in the other. What requires punishment in one world requires pardon in the other. Sweet is sour, black is white. Here Hegel says in the terms of ordinary speech and thought what he means by the "inverted world." The reader can see in common-sense terms that Hegel means a second world in which black is white, criminals are benefactors. This is both an inverse and a perverse world because not only is our ability to know the nature of the world inverted, our ability to know our own nature as moral agents is perverted.

Hegel holds his discursive and common-sense ways of speaking together by the overall image of the *verkehrte Welt.* The power of what Hegel is describing conceptually comes from this image, this *Bild,* that allows us to hold the phenomenon before our eyes. The English term "topsy-turvy" is an apt word for this image. The first element of the English word is related to "top" and the second to "to turn over." Topsy-turvy is the top where the bottom should be; the object is reversed. Hegel could agree with Addison's use of the term in his sentence: "I found nature turned topsy-turvey, women changed into men, and men into women." [12] There is no term that fully translates *verkehrte Welt.* It is the topsy-turvy, reverse, inverse, perverse-inverse world.

In fact Hegel introduces the concept of the topsy-turvy world by a contrast between it and a second image—the tranquil kingdom of laws—mentioned above. This "tranquil kingdom" *(ruhiges Reich)* is turned topsy-turvy. What was *ruhig* becomes *unruhig*. Consciousness now finds itself in a topsy-turvy kingdom where fools flourish—where the north pole is the south, criminals are saints, men are women. What has happened in this image? Consciousness has lost its bearings, but how has it lost them? The chaos of the inverted world is due to the fact that the oppositions between the two supersensible worlds are *equal*. They are just reversals of each other. Fill in any particular content, say, black, and in the other world one finds in its place, white. And the reverse. Consciousness has lost the function of the double sense of the *Ansich* in which a direction to any opposition is present, in which there is a necessary movement from one sense of *Ansich* to the other *Ansich* for consciousness.

The chaos reigns because consciousness has seemingly lost its ability to see the unseen behind the seen. It has created an unseen, a supersensible, behind the seen, the appearance, that it cannot convert back into a new perspective on the seen. It has placed itself in a state in which anything is possible, in which things may be just as much one way as the other. Consciousness seems to have put itself in the position where it cannot produce its dialectical relationship with the object. To escape this consciousness has to realize that the evil genius that has come over it is a state of itself and not the true state of the world. The topsy-turvy world is ingenuity run wild, ingenuity performed for ingenuity's sake. Consciousness must realize that it itself is the reality behind this impossible state of affairs. When it does this, it can experience itself as something other than the thought of the object. It establishes itself as self-consciousness. When it does this, it grasps itself as a new *Ansich* that it then takes up as something for itself. The directionality of opposition is now reestablished.

The theme of reversal is a crucial one for Hegel. The reversal of identity is the life blood of the image as well as the dialectical concept. The speech of the image, of the mythic, religious, or aesthetic image, is one of changing identity. In the narrative behind the Eleusinian mysteries, the Hymn to Demeter, Demeter is said to have gone among men in disguise following the abduction of her daughter. When she arrived at Eleusis, Demeter was taken in by the king and put in charge of the care of his son. This son grew like a god because each day Demeter anointed him with ambrosia and each night held him in the fire. She is discovered and the process interrupted. Demeter reveals herself as a goddess. The unseen is seen. Having learned this secret, the secret of her identity, those of Eleusis can be taught Demeter's secrets, the secrets of the reversals of nature. If we think of this in terms of Christian doctrine, something that dominated Hegel's early consciousness, we recall that Jesus had a problem with his identity, with being recognized as the "holy of holies" (the supersensible) made flesh. Hyppolite says: "In the Sermon on the Mount, Christ repeatedly opposes appearance—'it has been said'—to profound reality—'I say unto you'. Hegel takes up this opposition of inner and outer and considers it in all its scope." [13]

Hegel uses the syllogism *(Schluss)* in this section as a means for structuring his presentation. The *verkehrte Welt* is not an argument but a presentation of the experience of reversal which consciousness must live through. The sense of the reversal of world order and the sense of the revelation of a beyond that exists as an inner within things is the natural province of metaphorical language or mythico-religious language. In the *Phenomenology* Hegel is struggling to transpose this power of the image (the power to hold together oppositions) into a particular type of conceptual power. The syllogism is a form that can accomplish this.

From the beginning of the chapter of "Force and Understanding" Hegel describes his problem solely in abstract terms (Miller 132–43). The reader is given no metaphor or example of what Hegel is referring to in our ordinary sense of experience such as he has provided in the previous two chapters. The reader feels as though he were in a kind of conceptual sleepwalking, knowing that he is in motion but not knowing where he is going. We finally arrive at the goal when Hegel speaks of a "play of Forces" and structures this distinction in terms of the syllogism (Miller, 143). The "thing" as the ground of perceptions of the object has been activated as a force field, a kind of monad which has an outer dimension as substance and an inner dimension that has no immediacy for consciousness. Hegel says: "This true essense of Things has now the character of not being immediately for consciousness; on the contrary, consciousness has a mediated relation to the inner being and, as the Understanding, *looks through this middle of the play of Forces into the true background of Things"* (Miller, 143).

In order to cope with this "play of Forces" consciousness creates a syllogism by making the "inner being" immediate and the "outer" or substance the supersensible. The syllogism that emerges has as its middle term appearance ("This 'being' is therefore called *appearance*." Miller, 143). Its other two terms that are joined through appearance are the supersensible world (what formally was "Force as Substance," Miller, 142) and the Understanding; ". . . there now opens up above the *sensuous* world, which is the world of *appearance,* a *supersensible* world which henceforth is the *true* world, above the vanishing *present* world there opens up a permanent *beyond* [das bleibendes *Jenseits*] " (Miller, 144). The relationship is now: supersensible Beyond—sensuous Appearance—the Understanding (Miller, 145).

Here we have reached the syllogism of Kant's first *Critique.* Hegel says: "What is *immediate* for the Understanding is the play of Forces; but what is the *True* for it, is the simple inner world" (Miller, 148). In an effort by the Understanding *(Verstand)* to form the connections of this syllogism, it turns the supersensible realm into the realm of laws: "Consequently, the *supersensible* world is an inert *realm of laws* which, though beyond the perceived world—for this exhibits law only through incessant change—is equally *present* in it and is its direct tranquil image" (Miller, 149). This is the notion of Newtonian science of mechanics carried to a total philosophy of the object.

But when consciousness expands its notion of law it realizes that the laws of the specific types of play in the play of Forces mean just that everything in the world of appearance is lawlike and in a total structure; all laws are unified in the notion of "universal attraction" *(allgemeine Attraktion)*. "Universal attraction merely asserts that *everything has a constant difference in relation to other things*" (Miller, 150). Hegel asserts that law is present in a "two-fold manner" (Miller, 152) in that it is the same as Force, Force that differentiates itself from itself, but then is drawn back into itself. Hegel's examples are electricity that acts as a positive and negative electricity and gravity that in different moments of motion and space are all related to one another as root and square (Miller, 152). "In the play of Forces this law showed itself to be precisely this absolute transition and pure change; the selfsame, viz. Force *splits* into an antithesis which at first appears to be an independent difference, but which in fact proves *to be none*" (Miller, 156).

It is in relation to this point that Hegel introduces the *verkehrte Welt*. The original version of the supersensible world was that it was an immediate copy of the perceived world. But when its laws are expressed as forces which split into differences that are not really differences but just their selfsame selves (Electricity *is* positive and negative electricity) then the Understanding enters the inverted world. A second supersensible world is created that is the inversion of the first. Hegel states this as: "According, then, to the law of this inverted world, what is *like* in the first world is *unlike* to itself, and what is *unlike* in the first world is equally *unlike to itself,* or it becomes *like itself*" (Miller, 158).

Since law is identical to a force we have here the situation where the Understanding has present to itself only two possibilities—two poles. We take the pole of positive electricity and the other is negative but we take the pole that was negative and the other is negative of it. Also electricity is something *both* positive and negative. It is both and neither. One is as equally real as the other. Electricity is both and neither; it is nothing in itself. We cannot fix the difference in a "sustaining element" (Miller, 160). "It is the opposite of an opposite" (ibid.). Dialectic here breaks down, because it can find no direction within the opposition. There can be no dialectical movement forward when consciousness is faced with finding its reality within a perfect standoff of two opposites. One is the *Verkehrung* of the other and the other is the *Verkehrung* of it and they are both somehow each other, both somehow the same thing.

Having attempted to follow to an extent Hegel's presentation, I wish to consider the general sense of the syllogism and the middle term that Hegel is using as he moves toward the syllogism of the final paragraph of the chapter (Miller, 165). As he introduces the idea of the "play of Forces" Hegel says our object is the syllogism: *"Our object* is herewith then the syllogism which has at its extremes the inner of things and the understanding and appearance at its middle; but the movement of this syllogism is the further determination of what the understanding catches sight of through the middle term in the inner and the experience that the understanding has concerning this relationship of being closed together" (Hoffmeister, pp. 111–12; Miller, 145—my trans.). In his *Wissenschaft der Logik* Hegel says that the essential feature of the syllogism is the middle term, the *medius terminus.*[14]

There are two ways to consider the structure of the syllogism, both of which can be traced to Aristotle.[15] One way, the best known of the two, is to regard the syllogism as a mode for the formal presentation of thought. It is a form in which thought expresses rigorously the judgments it knows to be true. The syllogism is an *instrument of demonstration.* The other way to regard the syllogism is as a framework for the generation of ideas. From this perspective it is an *instrument of intelligibility.* It describes the means whereby thought forms itself. In this second sense of the syllogism the middle term is all-important because it is the commonplace or *topos* out of which the other two terms are drawn forth. The syllogism as the form of the creation of thought begins not with the problem of properly arranging premises and conclusion but with the problem of creating premises—the problem of formulating an enthymeme and expanding it into a demonstration.

Hegel, in his *Lectures on the History of Philosophy,* says of Aristotle's *topoi:* "in them the points of view from which anything can be considered are enumerated. Cicero and Giordano Bruno worked this out more fully." [16] Hegel contrasts the Renaissance use of topics with that of Aristotle: "But the Topics of Aristotle did this [developed lists of common places] in order to apprehend and determine an object in its various aspects, while Bruno rather worked for the sake of lightening the task of memory." [17]

In this topical sense of the syllogism that was promoted in the Renaissance the middle term and the premises are aspects of a common process of the creation of thought. A commonplace or *topos* is brought to mind that the speaker and hearers have in common. On this basis a connection between two other terms is made that is not commonly present. The initial form that this often takes is the expression by the speaker of an enthymeme that contains the middle term and a suggestion of the premises involved. In this process thought has made an advance because it has brought forth from the *topos* of the middle term what was not evident to it. It does this by moving back upon the middle term and recalling to itself what is contained in its meaning. There is no method for the topical construction of syllogisms. It depends upon the ingenuity *(ingenium)* of the speaker to create an enthymeme which can be opened out into a full syllogism.

How does consciousness come by its syllogism of appearance as the middle term and understanding and the inner of the appearance as its two extreme terms? In the second chapter of the *Phenomenology* consciousness has established the middle term of appearance by the connection of perception and deception. In the third chapter consciousness has appearance before it as something in itself. Consciousness must bring forth from appearance the understanding and the inner of the appearance. The notion of appearance is necessary to make sense of the inner forces and the Understanding. Once consciousness loses this sense of appearance as an external to itself and to the object, it falls into the phenomenon of the inverted world. The appearance ceases to be a middle term and the Understanding takes over the object completely. Then appearance becomes just an opposing sense of the object as defined by the Understanding. Appearance loses its status as something truly external in itself and becomes wholly functional as an interpretation within understanding. Then understanding cannot establish a criterion out of itself to make one of its interpretations of the object the appearance and the other the reality. All is turned upside down. In fact there is no right-side-up.

As Hegel writes in the last paragraph of the chapter: "Raised above perception, consciousness exhibits itself closed in a unity with the supersensible world through the mediating term of appearance, through which it gazes into this background [lying behind appearance]. The two extremes [of this syllogism], the one, of the pure inner world, the other, that of the inner being gazing into this pure inner world, have now coincided, and just as they, *qua* extremes, have vanished, so too the middle term, as something other than these extremes, has also vanished" (Miller, 165). Hegel says that when this curtain of appearance is drawn away the result is two inners—that of the inner being of the object and that of the I. Consciousness has survived its nightmare of world inversion.

The syllogism of force and understanding is not a structure of three dialectical moments for consciousness. The middle term is the *topos,* the *Ansich* out of which the two extremes emerge as moments in which the *Ansich* of appearance is something for consciousness—the object as inner force of the appearance, the form in which the appearance is something for consciousness. And, the other extreme, the Understanding, is the force of universalizing this inner of the object as law. We discover in the end, as the above passage says, that these two inners are the same—they are the way the object as force is something for consciousness. The middle term never was a synthesis of two moments but an *Ansich* to be grasped by consciousness. The middle term disappears when the I as the merger of the two inners becomes a new *Ansich.*

II

(1) What is the origin of Hegel's metaphor of the *verkehrte Welt?* Readers of the *Phenomenology* usually presume it is Hegel's own term. The commentators never question it. To my knowledge, no commentator ever mentions the possibility that Hegel's *verkehrte welt* is connected with the play with the same name by Ludwig Tieck. In 1799, eight years before Hegel published the *Phenomenology,* Ludwig Tieck (the author of *Puss in Boots, Der Gestiefelte Kater*) published a play entitled *Die verkehrte Welt.* Tieck's play has two precursors. A source for Tieck's work, although minor in its influence on it, was a play by the same title, *Die verkehrte Welt,* by Christian Weise (1683). Another one-act play, *Verkehrte Welt,* by Johann Ulrich von König (1725), bears no real resemblance to Tieck's play. These plays have connection with the Italian *commedia dell'arte.*[18] One of the main characters in Tieck's play is Scaramuccio, also a character in König's play. One reason Hegel's commentators have not noticed the connection with Tieck's play is that it has remained obscure except to Tieck specialists. Another reason is that Hegel's commentators make little exploration of his interest in literature. A look into Tieck's play readily reveals that it concerns the kind of reversal of the order of things that concerns Hegel in the last pages of "Force and Understanding." There is no certainty that Hegel read Tieck's play, but he may have. The play was a unique and controversial work from its inception. Tieck's publisher, the rationalist C. F. Nicolai, refused to publish it, in a strong letter to Tieck that reminds one of the criticism often expressed from a common-sense viewpoint against abstract expressionist art, namely, that "anyone could do it! " Nicolai writes: "The eccentric is after all easy work. I do not know how much I could write down every day if I would write down all that comes into my head." [19]

Tieck wrote the play in 1797 and published the first version of it in *Bambocciaden* (1799), a miscellany edited by A. F. Berhnardi (Italian: *bambocciata, bambocceria,* childishness, silly action).[20] During Tieck's lifetime his play had a number of important admirers. Among them were the Schlegel brothers, William Grimm, Eichendorff, and Schleiermacher. Schleiermacher wrote to Henriette Herz that he had laughed long and hard on reading the play and that "Tieck is indeed peerless." [21] Tieck was a friend of the Schlegel brothers and contributed essays to the journal *Athenäum,* founded by Friedrich Schlegel in 1798. Tieck was part of the circle of the Schlegels at Jena just prior to Hegel's arrival there.[22] Friedrich Schlegel, who had become *Privatdozent* at Jena in 1796, and Tieck spent the winter of 1799–1800 together at Jena, the year in which Tieck's *Die verkehrte Welt* was published.[23] Hegel arrived early in 1801. In the general introduction to the *Lectures on Aesthetics,* Hegel comments on Tieck's irony and refers to the Jena period as the focal point for this aspect of Tieck.[24]

Hegel refers to the *verkehrte Welt* in the *Science of Logic,* using the same examples of the inversion of south and north pole, positive and negative electricity, and good and evil that he uses in the *Phenomenology.*[25]

In the idea of the *verkehrte Welt* Hegel may have Kant's phenomena-noumena distinction in mind, as Flay maintains. He may have in mind the status of the "general law of nature" as a problem in early modern science in Galileo and Newton, that has its original ground in the connection of *eidos* and the changeable appearance in ancient thought, in Plato and Aristotle, as Gadamer claims. The key to the dialectic of this section may be Christian Gospels and Hegel's moral examples of crime and punishment, as Hyppolite maintains. Each of these views throws light on the section. None of them fully excludes the others. I do not disagree with any of these views.

Attention to Tieck's play does not simply offer a thesis of where Hegel obtains the term *verkehrte Welt* but throws light on the section itself, not as a problem in the history of philosophy, but as an immediate existential condition of consciousness. Tieck's work dramatizes what consciousness feels at this point, as it goes into a swoon with its own analytic powers of understanding before it emerges as certain of the truth of its own existence as self. Each stage in the *Phenomenology* is not just a problem in thought often connected with problems in the history of philosophical and moral ideas; each stage is also an actual set of conditions of life through which consciousness is living.

What does Tieck's play show of these conditions? Tieck's play proceeds through a series of scenes that have no specific connection except continual ironic shifts of perspective. Tieck ironically subtitled his work "Ein historisches Schauspiel in fünf Aufzügen" (An historical drama in five acts").[26] The play begins upside down, with an Epilogue, and concludes with a Prologue. Here are some of the play's features as described by Oscar Mandel in the play's first and quite recent English translation (1978): "A fictive audience is shown on stage, watching a play on a fictive stage, this play being visible to both the fictive and real audiences."[27] This reminds one of Hegel's distinction between appearance (the actual play before both audiences) and the first and second supersensible worlds (the regular audience and the fictive one, both of which can change into each other). In the play "a fictive character—say Scaramuccio—can be given his own discrimination between what is fiction for him and what is real for him."[28] He can impersonate an actor. "A member of the fictive audience and one of the fictive actors decide to exchange roles."[29] "In the last act the fictive audience rises *en masse* in order to alter the action according to its own tastes." [30] Tieck's play is so complicated it has scarcely ever been performed.[31] Tieck's play is like a work of Pirandello.

The levels of reversal go further: "In the play the fictive audience is watching, the personages at one point sit down to watch a play, in which the personages once again gather to watch a play. The fictive audience is now in a whirl; the walls of reality seem to buckle; reality threatens to dissolve in dream; and one of the fictive spectators suddenly cries out, 'What if *we* were fiction too?' " [32] At the end of the play Prologue enters as a character in the play but finds the theatre empty, with all the actors behind the curtain. The final speech of the play is by Greenfeather *(Grün-helm)*, who says: "Ha! here was a whole Prologue directed at me, namely one of the chief personages in the play, and yet he remained completely unaware of my presence, and yet I'm the only person here! This is a marvel that deserves to be investigated by the philosophers." [33]

Consider Hegel's statement at the end of the chapter on Force and Understanding: "This curtain [*Vorhang*] [of appearance] hanging before the inner world is therefore drawn away, and we have the inner being [the 'I'] gazing into the inner world . . ." (Miller, 165).[34] Greenfeather says: "I'm the only person here! *[der einzige Mensch!]*." Hegel says all we have left is the selfsame I after the experience of the *verkehrte Welt*. The raising of this curtain is a "marvel that deserves to be investigated by the philosophers." And now it has.

(2) In his essay, "Die verkehrte Welt," Gadamer suggests that the *verkehrte Welt* is a central element for the whole Hegelian construction *(Aufbau)* of the *Phenomenology*.[35] I find this true. Quentin Lauer suggests that the idea of *verkehrte Welt* is tied to the project of speculative philosophy itself: "As Hegel sees it, then, understanding has been pushed into a corner, where its own concepts are not faithful reproductions but reverse images of the world as 'sound common sense' took it to be. In a letter to his friend van Ghert on December 18, 1812, Hegel puts the matter clearly and succinctly: 'To the uninitiated, speculative philosophy, as regards its content, must simply seem to be the world reversed *[die verkehrte Welt]*, contradicting all their habitual concepts and whatever else, according to so-called sound common sense, seemed to them valid." [36] There is a sense in which speculative philosophy pushes the "sound" interpretation of the world consciousness has secured for itself in any one of its moments "into a corner" and causes its world to reverse.

Each stage of consciousness begins in the certain hope that it has discovered the unity between the two moments of consciousness itself— the unity of being *an sich* and of being *für sich*. It lives for a while in the wonderful light, thinking that its alienation has been overcome, yet as it seeks to verify this to itself, it slowly becomes uncertain. As the uncertainty grows it becomes perverse in its attempt to hold to the unity it has discovered, and finally it becomes mad and wastes its substance, or at least what it believed its substance to be. In these final moments the world in which it lives is *verkehrt,* turned over, reversed in topsy-turvy fashion until its head swims. Momentarily it suffers the loss of its soul, then the illusion of the next form of unity, the next stage of its self-development appears. Nothing explicit is learned from this experience because, like the soul undergoing reincarnation, it forgets everything as it experiences the relief of the next solution to its internal separation. The joy of the new world it sees, the seeming solidity of it, eases the *Angst* of the *Verkehrung* from which it has emerged.

In the *Phenomenology,* the *verkehrte Welt* emerges as a stage just at the completion of the general stage of Consciousness. The *verkehrte Welt* marks the entrance to the general stage of Self-consciousness. At this turning point consciousness comes to its first reckoning. Consciousness brings forth from itself the principle by which it has developed as consciousness and which will be the basis for its further movement, a principle which it immediately forgets in the joy of the self-certainty it has produced with this.

The *verkehrte Welt* is one of those places, as I have said, that most of Hegel's commentators have avoided. It is more than just another transition in the *Phenomenology.* To understand the *verkehrte Welt* we must be aware that Hegel is drawing on an image from a tradition in German literature that goes back to the late Middle Ages (as well as, perhaps and more immediately, to Tieck's play). Gadamer mentions this tradition in a footnote to his essay but does not develop it beyond referring the reader to several works on this tradition.[37] Hegel intends more than literary irony in his use of the *verkehrte Welt,* and I think there is more at stake in this tradition itself than literary irony.

Ludwig Tieck's play has a genuine philosophical intent. Deep behind this play is the theme of the *verkehrte Welt* in German consciousness, especially as it exists at the beginning of the development of German consciousness. Karl Rosenkranz, in his *Geschichte der deutschen Poesie im Mittelalter* (History of German poetry in the middle ages), explains the theme of the *verkehrte Welt* in relation to two phenomena: the *Narrenschiff* or ship of fools and the *Totentanz* or dance of death.[38] The *Narrenschiff* (1494) was the first work of German world literature, written by Sebastian Brant in his own dialect and Early New High German, but rapidly translated into Latin and into most European languages[39] (and it is the basis for the modern novel, *Ship of Fools* [1962], by Katherine Anne Porter). The Grimm's *Deutsches Wörterbuch* cites Brant's *Narrenschiff* as a source for the verb *verkehren.*[40]

Brant's work treats of 112 different types of foolishness, ways in which one can falsely think or act, beginning with the folly of "useless books" and ending with the folly of "the wise man," and including along the way the foolishness of "blowing into ears" and "useless studying," to mention only two. The *Phenomenology* can be seen as a philosophical ship of fools, in which each stage is a different compartment in the ship, and the individual reader, following the original course of the illusions of consciousness itself, works his way toward wisdom. A fool gets reality backwards and takes illusion for reality. This can cut him off from the true perception of the divine and the salvation of his own soul. From Brant's work we can learn the various types of *Verkehrungen* that engage fools and how to seek our own salvation. Both Hegel and Brant are authors who deliberately shock the reader. In remarking on the power of the *verkehrte Welt* to shock the reader, Gadamer says: "Hegel is a Swabian and shocking people is his passion, as it is the passion of all Swabians." [41]

The Ship of Fools and the Dance of Death are strong original images in German consciousness. The Ship of Fools, like the Dance of Death, was not simply a literary work but an actual practice, a practice Foucault has described in his *Histoire de la Folie*. Foucault says: "the Ship of Fools, a strange 'drunken boat' that glides along the calm rivers of the Rhineland and the Flemish canals . . . for they did exist, these boats that conveyed their insane cargo from town to town. . . . Often the cities of Europe must have seen these 'ships of fools' approaching their harbors." [42] Foucault says most towns drove fools outside their limits and that "the custom was especially frequent in Germany." [43] Of the fool's situation, Foucault says: "He is the Passenger *par excellence:* that is, the prisoner of the passage. And the land he will come to is unknown—as is, once he disembarks, the land from which he comes." [44] Are we not the "prisoner of the phenomenological passage" ? As Hegel says in the Preface to the *Phenomenology:* "When natural consciousness entrusts itself straightway to Science, it makes an attempt, induced by it knows not what, to walk on its head too, just this once . . . relatively to immediate self-consciousness it *[Wissenschaft]* presents itself in an inverted posture *[als ein Verkehrtes]* " (Miller, 26; Hoffmeister, p. 25).

The Dance of Death involves the *verkehrte Welt* because it places life in the mirror of its opposite. The *Totentanz* figures in a number of early poetic works and paintings but is not the subject of a single work equal to the *Narrenschiff*.[45] Death dances with each person. It affects equally Pope, king, and child. The Dance of Death inverts our sense of what is real from what is here to what is beyond and thus makes uncertain our "sound common sense" apprehension of things. I quote from an early discourse with Death, *Der Ackermann aus Böhmen (The Plowman from Bohemia),* written by Johannes von Saaz in 1401: "the earth and all that therein is are built upon transience. In our day they have become unsettled, for all things have been reversed *[alle ding haben sich verkeret]*, the last has become the first, the first has become the last, what was below has risen above and what was above has fallen below. The greater part of people has turned wrong into right." [46] This portrait of *Verkehrung* is not far from Hegel's inversion of north and south polarities and of good and bad. In another place Death says: "Fools call good what is wicked, and wicked what is good." [47]

The relationship of death and the fool is complex. Death can appear as a fool wearing the fool's costume, cap, and scepter, who drags off the human fool, the lump who once wore them. William Willeford, in his study of fools, says: "According to a late medieval conceit, Death, himself a fool, makes fools of us all . . . the fool survives his own death: abandoning the *prima materia* of the human image, the fool enters the dimension in which Harlequin once led a horde of ghosts. A similar form of immortality is implied when the circus clown jumps to his feet after having been hit over the head with a sledge hammer." [48] The fool survives his inversion of things and, like consciousness at the end of the *verkehrte Welt* experience, he survives as an *I* on a different plane. Rosenkranz says: "the Dance of Death exposes to view the claim the fool's world has on us and inverts the inversion *[verkehrt ihre Verkehrung]*." [49] The dance of Death is a *Verkehrung* of the fool in us; it is both a kind of folly—the celebration of death in life—and the element of self-correction in folly that opens us to another plane of existence. Consciousness is thrown back upon itself and the problem of its own reality and truth. "Death," as Hegel says, "is of all things the most dreadful . . ." (Miller, 32). Rosenkranz says: "Death, that which runs counter to the human being, brings his foolishness into consciousness for him." [50] The specter of death concentrates the mind wonderfully.

Why is the *verkehrte Welt* so important to the *Phenomenology?* The answer to this must be sought in the character of German consciousness itself. In raising the specter of the *verkehrte Welt* Hegel is dealing with the greatest *Angst* that is at the basis of German culture. It is an *Angst* that is present in human consciousness generally, but if considered within the context of German consciousness its meaning for German philosophy can be highlighted. German life is famous for its interest in *Ordnung* (order). The orderliness of German life is impressive and the interest in order is reflected in the common expressions "Alles muss in Ordnung sein" ("Everything must be in order"), "Alles in Ordnung" ("All in order"), and "Ordnung muss sein" ("Order must be"). What can be seen in these expressions of everyday life is reflected on the intellectual level with the famous concern of German thought with *Wissenschaft*—the attainment in a subject matter of objective, systematic order of its contents. What is *unwissenschaftlich,* like what is *unordentlich,* counts for very little.

Wissenschaft is essentially a sense of system but it need not be a functional system. To have *Wissenschaft* present to the mind it is necessary only that logical distinctions be made and things are ordered into a scheme. The scheme need not be functional in the sense of the distinctions operating in relation to each other so that we can see how it would act or how such a set of distinctions would produce a result. The order of the scheme itself is satisfying. A scheme of order done on a subject matter or an area of experience done in high seriousness with intent on objective order is sufficient.

What is *Ordnung* in life or *Wissenschaft* in thought an answer to? What is the problem that *Ordnung* in all affairs of life and the *Ordnung* of *Wissenschaft* is attempting to solve? What is the phenomenon in the experience of consciousness to which *Wissenschaft* is the response? It is the possibility that experience is meaningless. What if, despite all our efforts to assure ourselves of meaning through the presentation of order, actuality (what is *wirklich*), is the opposite of our systems? What if Descartes' *malin génie* is valid? What if the world is in principle exactly the opposite of what it so clearly seems to be? What if, after having heard the explanation of reality of the *Wissenschaftler,* and in answer to the question *Alles klar?,* our thoughts turn to the possibility of the *verkehrte Welt?* How can we know that in our search for authoritative knowledge that we or other *Wissenschaftler* are not guilty *(schuldig)* of leaving some stone unturned? How can we provide against the possibility that, try as we will to have experience make sense *(Sinn),* our understandings may in fact be systematic nonsense *(Unsinn)?* All our quest for *Sinn* may in reality be simply *Wahnsinn*—madness, insanity. Despite all the activity of the *Geisteswissenschaften* and the *Naturwissenschaften*, the guilt remains. The doubt remains that something in principle can be wrong.

The only answer to the *verkehrte Welt,* this hobgoblin, is a *Wissenschaft* of the experience of consciousness that can in principle overcome the possibility that things are not in reality what they seem to the powers of the Understanding. Kant has failed to do this in his concept of *Wissenschaft* just because it is tied to a *Wissenschaft* of the Understanding *(Verstand)*. Kant's *Critiques* are heroic attempts to fulfill the desire of classical *Wissenschaft*—to make a set of distinctions so powerful that all of experience is defined by them. But Kant has left the stone of the noumenal unturned. He confesses this fact from the beginning of his system. And he has within his system of the phenomenal world of experience left his table of categories without a self-deriving foundation. The categories just arrive for us via logic (specifically Meier's logic) but without our knowing how logic is grounded in the real.

Philosophy must have the high place it does in German culture because no special *Wissenschaft* can satisfy the *Angst* expressed in the *verkehrte Welt,* that our ordering of experience may in principle be defective, that we may be living in a perfectly ordered or orderable world but a world that is topsy-turvy. Hegel realizes the importance of commanding the idea of *Wissenschaft* from the start when he entitles the *Phenomenology* the first part of his *System der Wissenschaft* (see below, Appendix). What is required is a science that commands *absolutes Wissen*. Hegel, in a Promethean act, steals the name *Wissenschaft* right from the hands of the special sciences and claims it only for philosophy, the true form of thought. Consciousness can overcome its fundamental *Angst* only if it can live through all its possible *Verkehrungen,* its worst (and its best) illusions as stages of itself on a pathway that produces as its end absolute knowing. Hegel plays with the worst fears and undertakes the labor of the negative *(Arbeit des Negativen)* (Hoffmeister, p. 20; Miller, 19). Hegel "stares the negative in the face" (Hoffmeister, p. 30; Miller, 32). No specific field of study or philosophy that depends upon the power of the Understanding to make distinctions, even fundamental distinctions, can overcome the possibility that "alles ist falsch." To overcome this possibility, a totally new sense of system which displays the self-development of consciousness is necessary, one based on *Vernunft.*

Does Hegel succeed with his new sense of *Wissenschaft* in allaying the *Angst* that all in principle may yet be false to being? Any reader will have to judge for himself. His judgment must depend upon whether the possession of Hegel's famous "absolute" is also the possession of being itself. Is being fully within the Hegelian *System der Wissenschaft* or not? Heidegger's theme of *Angst* can be seen to have its roots here. If an ontological difference between *Sein* and *Seindes* remains after the Hegelian attempt at the perfect *Wissenschaft,* we have not been freed from the original, primordial threat of the *verkehrte Welt.* Representational thinking can never free us from this possibility that resides directly in our separation from Being, a condition that resides in human existence itself.

Hegel's own ironic and comedic-tragic approach to existence gives way to the dead serious attending to Being. Heidegger's own personal recurrent dream, that he is asked questions by his school examiners and cannot find the answer, is also ours.[51] We must put any sense of humor or folly of the human condition aside. We are engaged in a sophisticated *Totentanz* in which we realize that the only answer to the specter of the *verkehrte Welt* is Being itself. The meditative activity of *das Denken* is what is open to us until Being comes to us.[52] The apprehension of Being for us is simply uncertain. As Heidegger said, in words he arranged to have published after his death, we may have to wait three hundred years until the proper form of meditative thinking can take effect.[53]

Hegel has begun his treatment of consciousness and at the same time his treatment of the whole experience of consciousness with an ironic pun on *das Meinen.* Hegel begins the *Phenomenology* with a joke and he ends the first part of it, the treatment of Consciousness, with a joke—the irony of the topsy-turvy world. In between these jokes moves Hegel's account of the first part of the science of the experience of consciousness. Consciousness is in its first moment moved further by the "divine nature" of language to double meaning. It is moved to the standpoint of self-consciousness by the power of language systematically to double itself into two complete worlds of meaning, one the reverse of the other. Now the power of language must be re-learned so that it becomes the speech of the I.

Five

Masterhood and Servitude

Hegel's metaphor of masterhood and servitude, his portrait of the *Herr* (master) and the *Knecht* (servant), is the most memorable section of the *Phenomenology*. Once read, it is impossible to forget. It is a memory image that stretches out in all directions and allows the reader to recall his own struggles of existence. Suddenly the reader feels he can make some sense of the webs, the entanglements, he has felt himself to be in. The *we* that is observing the process of consciousness in the stages of the *Phenomenology* takes on a new attitude of alertness as to what it may learn from its regard of this development. Hegel gives the *we* a new reason to keep awake at just the point where the passivity involved in knowing the object had allowed the *we* to believe it was really just an observer.

Hegel's metaphor of *Herrschaft* and *Knechtschaft* is both a political and a psychological image. It can excite both Marxist and Fascist interest— Marxist because of the role of work, Fascist because of Hegel's sense of death and the implications this could have for the power of war over the individual and the dominance of the state. The psychologist becomes interested because of the role of fear in the confrontation of the self with the other. What can be said about this metaphor, a metaphor through which the reputation of the *Phenomenology* is practically made? I wish to approach this section in two ways: (1) I wish to follow what Hegel says, with some emphasis on the connection of this section to the *verkehrte Welt;* (2) I wish to draw out implications of this section for an understanding of a praxis of individual existence, including the praxis of the individual philosopher's existence. In pursuing both these points I wish to understand what Hegel means by desire *(Begierde)*, life *(Leben)*, recognition *(Aner-kennen)*, death *(Tod)*, fear *(Furcht)*, and work *(Arbeit)*.

Hegel's presentation of masterhood and servitude is preceded by general remarks on the "Truth of Self-Certainty" ("Die Wahrheit der Gewissheit seiner selbst"). Hegel begins this fourth chapter of the *Phenomenology* with a reminder of what I have called his two senses of *Ansich* or double *Ansich*—the object apprehended as in itself and this in itself apprehended as something for consciousness. In Part A, "Consciousness," of the *Phenomenology,* natural consciousness has been caught in a motion that passes between these two senses of the object, with the object grasped as an external. This finally results in the syllogism of appearance and the upside-down world of the understanding. Hegel also reminds us that in knowing the concept and object correspond (Miller, 166).

In its three attempts—as sense, perception, and understanding—consciousness has been unable to bring the two moments of *Ansich* together.[1] All has ended in failure because these two moments cannot both be apprehended as a function of the object. The correspondence that has been sought between a world of laws and the appearance fails, and fails in a very large manner, in the motion sickness of the topsy-turvy world. Consciousness now gives up the certainty of the object for the certainty of itself. In doing so "certainty gives place to truth" (166). Natural consciousness now will try to place both senses of the *Ansich* within the boundaries of itself as knower. The first sense of *Ansich* that attracted natural consciousness toward the object is seen as a kind of something *for consciousness* that is different from this something as it is truly for consciousness (the second moment), as it comes fully under its power. This will end in failure. No real correspondence will be achieved between concept and object. Consciousness will now struggle with the object as an other of itself.

Hegel says: "With self-consciousness, then, we have therefore entered the native realm of truth" ("in das einheimische Reich der Wahrheit eingetreten") (Miller, 167; Hoffmeister, p. 134). Hegel has introduced the second part of the *Phenomenology* with an irony which is tied both to the ironic pun of *das Meinen* that begins the first part of the *Phenomenology* and the irony of the inverted world that ends it. Hegel's phrase, "native realm of truth," I believe, is meant to echo a special paragraph in Kant's first *Critique*. It is the only place in which Kant speaks poetically in the *Critique*—his introductory passage to the distinction of all objects in general into phenomena and noumena. Kant says:

> We have now not merely explored the territory of pure understanding, and carefully surveyed every part of it, but have also measured its extent, and assigned to everything in it its rightful place. This domain is an island, enclosed by nature itself within unalterable limits. It is the land of truth—enchanting name!—surrounded by a wide and stormy ocean, the native home of illusion, where many a fog bank and many a swiftly melting iceberg give the deceptive appearance of farther shores, deluding the adventurous seafarer ever anew with empty hopes, and engaging him in enterprises which he can never abandon and yet is unable to carry to

completion. Before we venture on this sea, to explore it in all directions and to obtain assurance whether there be any ground for such hopes, it will be well to begin by casting a glance upon the map of the land which we are about to leave, and to enquire, first, whether we cannot in any case be satisfied with what it contains—are not, indeed, under compulsion to be satisfied, inasmuch as there may be no other territory upon which we can settle; and, secondly, by what title we possess even this domain, and can consider ourselves as secured against all opposing claims.[2]

Kant's phrases here are "das Land der Wahrheit," "land of truth," and surrounded by "dem eigentlichen Sitze des Scheins," "the native home of illusion." Kant says that the territory of the pure understanding is the "land of truth" or, in other words, what Kant has explored in the course of the Analytic. The "native home of illusion" that surrounds it is the territory of the Dialectic. As Kant says in the first sentence of the Dialectic, dialectic is the *"logic of illusion" (Schein)*.[3] This is what results when reason attempts to take up the whole construction of the object of the Analytic as an object of its consciousness. This is the stormy ocean and fog that surrounds the land of truth, the island of the Analytic. Kant says that this may tempt us to adventure and to engage in enterprises we cannot complete. I am reminded here of Descartes' comment in the *Discours,* that those who give attention to the kind of thinking in *historie* and *fable* are "liable to fall into the extravagances of knights-errant of Romance, and form projects beyond their power of performance." [4]

As we have seen, the *Bildungsroman* of the *Phenomenology* is a doctrine of illusion *(Schein)*. We are in Kant's native home of illusion and Hegel's native realm of truth. We are on board Hegel's *Narrenschiff,* circling out ever wider from the island of the Understanding in the waters of the absolute. These are uncharted waters and we need always the power of the fool, the power to reverse the world, to turn the truth of understanding upside down to see its truth. The art of the fool is the art of world-reversal. Each stage of consciousness is a cabin in Hegel's *Narrenschiff.* Consciousness is continually caught in its own tomfoolery. Each stage is a Tom Fool, a Hodge, that is saved by its own power to reverse itself and that is ultimately saved by the power of the whole to draw the part on toward the peace of an *Entsprechung* between thought and object in absolute knowing. At each stage the *Phenomenology* is a comedy, a part of the *Narrenschiff,* but the true is the achievement of the whole. The whole is a tragedy. But through tragedy is won a kind of peace. It is a peace of the whole like that of which Hegel speaks in the bacchanalian revel—a transparent unbroken calm.

To return from this digression, what has Hegel done with Kant here? First, he has reversed Kant's metaphor of the land of truth. Truth is not the understanding, the stage out of which consciousness has just emerged, but the passing beyond understanding to the self-consciousness thought. This latter is instead the land of truth or native home of truth. Second, Hegel's ironic reversal has a reference back to the pun on *das Meinen*. The world of meaning or *Meinen* that has been achieved by consciousness as understanding is now superseded by a new truth of the *mein* of mine. In the stage of self-consciousness a new sense of mine is born. Consciousness now becomes active in relation to the object. Consciousness enters into a new sense of possession that is active, not passive.

This sense of mine is desire. Hegel says: "self-consciousness is *Desire* in general" (Miller, 167). The active stance that consciousness has assumed as self-consciousness is that of desiring. It strives to make the object of sense-certainty mine. Hegel says: "Consciousness, as self-consciousness, henceforth has a double object: one is the immediate object, that of sense-certainty and perception, which however *for self-consciousness* has the character of a *negative;* and the second, viz. *itself,* which is the true *essence,* and is present in the first instance only as opposed to the first object" (ibid.). Mine as desire is not the attempt at a "meaning," a *Meinen,* but at a real mine. It is not that consciousness takes up the object as its own and in some sense leaves the object there as an external ground of meaning. Consciousness acts to eliminate the object as something outside itself. Through desire, consciousness, as self-consciousness, hopes to overcome the double sense of the object—the double *Ansich.* This theme of doubleness runs throughout this section on self-consciousness and is not comprehensible without the interpretation I have previously advanced of the method of *Ansich.*

Hegel says: "Through this reflection into itself the object has become Life" (Miller, 168). What does Hegel mean here by life *(Leben)?* The object becomes a flow of shapes that is like the flow of moments of sense-certainty. A similar problem exists for self-consciousness as existed for consciousness as sense-certainty. Self-consciousness must differentiate within this flux, this medium. It must fix a meaning within the medium. Hegel says: "Life in the universal fluid medium, a *passive* separating-out of the shapes becomes, just by so doing, a movement of those shapes or becomes Life as a *process.* The simple universal fluid medium is the *in-itself,* and the difference of the shapes is the *other.* But this fluid medium itself becomes the *other* through this difference; for now it is *for the difference* which exists in and for itself, and consequently is the ceaseless movement by which the passive medium is consumed: Life as a *living thing*" (Miller, 171; Hoffmeister, p. 137).

We have here (1) the fluid medium *(flüssiges Medium* or *Flüssigkeit)* in which (2) here is a separating-out *(Auseinanderlegen)* of shapes *(Gestalten).* This medium stands to its shapes as *in-itself* to *other.* We now look back and see that the medium is the other since it is the medium of these differentiated shapes. It exists *for the difference.* It exists for the purpose of the difference. This element of difference is in and for itself and is an infinite moment as it causes *unendliche Bewegung.* Life exists as something *Lebendiges.* The difference *(Unterschied)* is a meta-element.

To understand what Hegel is talking about here let us follow the procedure of the *Republic* and write in larger letters what Hegel has written in smaller letters. Life exists as a total flow—concrete process. Culture is separated out from Life as shapes. Life is an in-itself. Culture, the world of shapes, is an other. Culture is alienated from Life. Its shapes are in fact shapes of Life. It must return to Life as the immediacy of its own non-immediacy. Life is now the other. Culture is something and Life is opposed to it. But then it is seen that Life exists *to become* culture. Life exists *for the difference.* Note that no synthesis has been achieved here. Life is opposed to culture. But culture turned upside down is life. And life turned upside down is culture.

To return to the smaller letters, life and shapes are opposed. But life is, on the other hand, just the generation of shapes or it is nothing, and the shapes are themselves nothing but the formations of life. The eternal element is the difference "which exists in and for itself." This difference must become a new in-itself if life is to become living *(lebendig).* This difference must become the object and work of consciousness as self-consciousness. Hegel says: "This *topsy-turvy,* however, is for that reason again *topsy-turviness in its own self*" (Miller, 171). In the original the sentence is: "Diese *Verkehrung* aber ist darum wieder die *Verkehrtheit an sich selbst*" (Hoffmeister, p. 137). The way out of this topsy-turviness of *Ansich* and *Andere* here is for consciousness to take up this *Verkehrtheit* as the mode of its being. In doing so it has a glimpse of infinity as ceaseless movement. The in and for itself of difference becomes a new in-itself that can now be for consciousness from within it—a stance of its life.

Hegel's use of *Verkehrung* and *Verkehrtheit* here refers the reader back to the metaphor of the *verkehrte Welt* that expressed the downfall of understanding. Consider the parallel (see Miller, 157). In understanding we have the perceived world (Life) and its laws that copy it in a supersensible fashion (shapes). The law was the selfsame element that supplied the constancy of the object for perception. But it is then realized that the object itself must be selfsame or the law could not be the copy of this selfsameness. Now there is a supersensible world on the side of the knower and one on the side of the object. One is just the opposite of the other. The middle term of appearance falls away.

There is no longer anything to refer to as that which the kingdom of laws copies or is like. In order to keep knower and known apart so that they do not collapse into simple identity, consciousness must regard one world as the simple opposite of the other. Now it falls into the well of deception. It enters the land of upside-down, of illusion. The object may just as well be thought to be white as black. The principle of change and alteration that was formerly within appearance has been taken on by the kingdom of laws and proposes to drive it mad. Instead of discovering the laws that account for the differences between men and women, the genetic sexual code, the understanding must now explain why men are not women and women not men. This is a task beyond its powers and it enters not a bacchanalian whirl but a nightmare of ratiocination. This antinomous existence makes consciousness long for the blessed isle of Kant's Analytic of the understanding and regret the day it dared to leave the middle term of appearance behind for its fog banks of illusion. Only when consciousness realizes that it itself is the author of this reversing of itself, does it leave, as Hegel says, "the nightlike void of the supersensible beyond, and steps out into the spiritual daylight of the present" (Miller, 177).

We who are watching Hegel's philosophical version of Tieck's play, we the audience, are also relieved because we see the dialectical movement go forward to the self, as we know it must. But we should not be relieved too quickly. For how did consciousness move on to self-consciousness? It may have moved just like one of the scenes in Tieck's play—another scene was just begun by the actors without transition. The "curtain of appearance" was drawn away and there was the *I* standing on the stage. All was accomplished for us by Hegel acting as a stage hand, quickly setting the new scene and ripping upwards the curtain to show us a new wonder before we could think there was a flaw in the script.

In fact I think Hegel does just this. But I do not think we should find this a defect in Hegel's account. It is only problematic for those who would interpret Hegel's dialectic in the *Phenomenology* as based in the deductive or rational-explanatory powers of language and thought. If we understand from the start that language has a poetic-presentational power through which the real is also shown, we can grasp how the "transition" for consciousness to self-consciousness is made. In fact, once this is seen, it is surprising that we should ever have expected otherwise. There are two kinds of speaking: (1) one kind of speech proceeds from a ground. It draws out of this established ground the meanings that are in it. In logic this is the deduction of propositions from axioms. But logic is just an example of this showing from a ground. (2) A second kind of speech brings forth the ground itself. This kind of speech is something that philosophers use but seldom like to talk about. It is mythic or poetic speaking. To have a beginning point for thought requires a metaphor. Metaphors are not derived. They are originals. The mind simply goes into itself and brings them forth. It *recollects* them from all of human culture that lies dormant within the collective unconscious of each mind. Such speech is like a new perception. The mind sees something it had not seen. When the metaphor comes forth, it has been in mind all the time but was not explicitly there for mind as a ground of its deliberate activity.

Ernesto Grassi, in his study of imagination and metaphor in Western thought, *Die Macht der Phantasie* (The power of imagination), points out that Hegel, in his *Lectures on Aesthetics,* regards the metaphor and the image *(Bild)* as allowing the real to remain only in individual form.[5] The immediacy of the metaphorical formation of the object in a *Bild* must be *aufgehoben* in the reflective thought of the *Begriff.* In this view Hegel represents the traditional understanding of the metaphor, Grassi holds, as something that does not command an essential place in knowing as opposed to an element that remains in the act of knowing and to which knowing must always return to forge its new beginning points.

Grassi says: "The question concerning the role of metaphor is whether metaphor represents in philosophical language only a remnant of sense apprehension that must be taken up and annulled on the way to *logos.*"[6] Grassi's answer is no. The view of metaphor that I am applying to Hegel's procedure in the *Phenomenology* derives from Grassi's view that the real always appears to us through metaphorical speech and the original meaning the metaphor bears is never cancelled or surpassed in the logical development of the word. Neither Grassi nor I are misologists. The problem is not the overcoming of logic. The problem is the re-understanding of what the ancients knew—the sense in which the metaphorical or mythic power of language is constantly required, and in fact is constantly employed, by the rational.[7] We see this pattern of employment throughout the *Phenomenology* and it offers insights into what Hegel is conceptually saying.

The metaphor always gives us a new sense of things. This is exactly what is required at the beginning of any stage of Hegel's *Phenomenology.* Hegel begins the stage of consciousness per se with the metaphor of *Das Meinen.* It comes to mind out of nowhere but out of itself. It is just drawn forth. Consciousness speaks. This is the ground for all else that is drawn forth throughout the stage of consciousness (Part A) in the *Phenomenology.* This ground reaches its limits. It wears itself out. Fatigue occurs. We are tired of hearing about the *meaning* of the object. We are tired of seeing it. We begin to go to sleep. Consciousness begins to go to sleep, only to find itself suddenly in the *verkehrte Welt,* to find suddenly a world of thoughts walking around on their hands with feet in the air, then righting themselves only to do more handsprings. The speech of consciousness that has drawn on the original pun of *Das Meinen* has exhausted itself and language must speak again from the same perspective as it originally did. It must simply speak forth a new ground.

In the metaphor of the topsy-turvy world this has already been done. Hegel draws from this metaphor the first steps of consciousness as self-consciousness in his explanation of desire and life, as I have discussed. The completion of this metaphor of the upside-down world is masterhood and servitude. Master and servant is the founding of the I present in the metaphor of the topsy-turvy world. We find Hegel speaking of the master-servant difference in terms of the *verkehrte Welt*. Hegel says: "But just as masterhood showed that its essential nature is the reverse *[das Verkehrte]* of what it wants to be, so too servitude in its consummation will really turn into the opposite of what it immediately is" (Miller, 193; Hoffmeister, p. 147). The whole section on Self-Consciousness of the *Phenomenology* is an especially rich section of metaphors. If we see that Hegel requires here a speech of the ground, not a speech of deduction, we can make good sense of a comment of Marx, a view that is perfectly correct. In the Third Manuscript of the *Economic and Philosophical Manuscripts* Marx says: "It is necessary to begin with the *Phenomenology,* because it is there that Hegel's philosophy was born and that its secret is to be found." [8] And further, in *The Holy Family:* "The whole of *Phenomenology* is intended to prove that *self-consciousness* is the *only reality* and *all reality.*" [9]

Although this is intended as a criticism, it is correct. There is a sense in which the stage of self-consciousness is a founding speech for the project of the *Phenomenology* as a whole and for Hegel's whole orientation of thought. The basic sensibility upon which all of Hegel's system is built is the struggle of a thing with itself. It makes sense that the metaphors of this part of Hegel's work should be the most striking—*verkehrte Welt, Herr und Knecht, unglückliches Bewusstsein.*

The lack of transition in deductive terms between consciousness and self-consciousness, or between any two stages where there is a new grounding in the *Phenomenology,* should also not surprise us. There is no transition in any deductive sense between the original two moments of the *Ansich,* upon which all spirit depends. One moment simply follows on the other with necessity. But there is no principle of relationship between them. Hegel's conception of the *Ansich* and the *Ansich* as something for consciousness is a conception of how explicit form is drawn forth from a ground. The metaphor is a new beginning point because it announces itself as a new identity between the two moments of the *Ansich.* Any metaphor, which, as Vico says, is a fable in brief, is a version of the object and of the object as available for consciousness. It is a subjective-object. The metaphor is thus a beginning point because the two levels of *Ansich* appear to be held together in it. As consciousness proceeds from this ground it must make articulate the sense of the two moments that are originally within it.

As consciousness proceeds with this conceptual process, supplemented with sub-metaphors along the way, the original metaphor, the beginning, is worn out. It loses all its power. But the *Begriff* has enriched itself with this *Bild* and drawn power from it. The *Begriff* comes to an end point, where it once again requires the ingenuity of the *Bild* to renew its own dialectical ingenuity. Hegel continually employs these two powers of speech against each other, as does consciousness itself in its actual structuring of the world. Carl Vaught says in *The Quest for Wholeness:* "Thus Hegel not only uses metaphors within his system as a way of enriching his thought, but also introduces a concept which is presupposed in their construction and which serves as the ground of both metaphorical representation and dialectical reflection." [10]

We can expect consciousness to move as suddenly from one major stage of its being to another as consciousness moves from one side of the in-itself to the other. Just as this double *Ansich* is a bond of necessity, so the doubling of consciousness itself into self-consciousness is a bond of necessity. This action simply *happens.* It happens through the bringing forth of a metaphor from the memory of consciousness. This metaphor is given conceptual life through the movement that ensues.

(2) I wish now to turn to my second point, that of the metaphor of master-servant itself, understood as a structure of praxis. Thus understood it is both a political and psychological structure. Hegel compares self-consciousness to the syllogism of the play of forces of Force and Understanding, where the inner being of things and the Understanding are the two extremes and the middle term is appearance (Miller, 145). I have characterized this in the preceding chapter as depending upon a topical sense of the syllogism. Here in relation to self-consciousness this is even more obvious. Hegel says: "The middle term is self-consciousness which splits into the extremes" (Miller, 184). Out of self-consciousness, out of the I, come the extremes of the I as a center of active resistance and the I as a center of active control. These two I's recognize *(Anerkennen)* each other. The middle term of the inner being of the I falls away and these two senses of self face off from each other. This splitting up is unequal: "one being only *recognized,* the other only *recognizing*" (Miller, 185).

This is a dangerous situation because the sense of the middle, the sense of the center has been lost. There is no natural *topos* or place, no common ground through which both of these I's can live their lives. Recognition here does not mean a high spiritual experience but an *acknowledgement* that the other is there in the world as a force to be dealt with. Each seeks the death of the other. Each engages in the risk of self-sacrifice. Hegel says: "it is only through staking one's life that freedom is won" (Miller, 187). There is a struggle that can have three outcomes: (1) the individual may shy away from the struggle. Hegel says the individual who does this may be recognized as a *person* but "he has not attained to the truth of this recognition" (ibid.). The self as person can command no genuine respect. (2) The individual may simply die. He can then become one of the honored dead. But this only shows he has missed the point of the action. The point is to survive this struggle. (3) The third possibility is to survive this struggle and learn the secret of freedom.

The fact that the self requires the risk of its own being on behalf of something beyond itself—freedom—is the basis of war in political life. It is also the basis of social disruption. When this drive for self-risk has no

outlet in war, it creates the conditions of war in order to attain itself—
to solve the problem of its own reality. There is no conceptual or organi-
zational solution to war because the risk of death, the actual risk of life
by a self, is a route by which the self solves the problem of its own
reality—comes to know that it is real. This is not simply risk because it
must be risk on behalf of freedom, what the self must attain in order to
be more than a mere person. I have discussed this question in another
place and will not go further with it here.[11] An honorable death is also
not the purpose of war; as Hegel says, the purpose is to survive, to survive
the risk of self. One's name on the list of the honored dead in the town
square is evidence of failure, not success. And to be a hero of the revolution
is to win it, not to be consumed by it.

If this struggle of the self to risk its own being to be itself, to realize
its own truth, is not drawn up into war but takes place within a stable
social framework, then one of the senses in which it can be understood is
as a structure of philosophical praxis. It can be seen as a portrait of the
List der Vernunft, of the cunning of reason, understood as actual cunning.
Like the returner to Plato's cave, the philosopher knows he must be very
clever if he is to stay alive. The *Herr,* the master or lord, is allowed to
dominate. The self appears to take on the cloak of servitude to this *Herr-
self.* The *Herr* soon discovers that it can live off of this *Knecht-self.* The
Herr soon learns to enjoy its life and in so doing it misses the experience
of fear *(Furcht).* The *Knecht* sees what the *Herr* misses: "For this consciousness has been fearful, not of this or that particular thing or just at
odd moments, but its whole being has been seized with dread *[Angst]*
(Miller, 194). The servant has seen what the master has not—that affairs
can reverse themselves. He learns what Boethius learns in *The Consolation
of Philosophy,* that: "Ill is it to trust Fortune's fickle bounty." [12] He allows
the master to continue his false sense of reality while he, the servant,
develops his tragic sense of existence. The experience of fear that is really
Angst has taught the servant the nothingness of things. It has in fact taught
him the nothingness of the master. The master depends upon him. At most
the master experiences a kind of uneasiness about his reality that leads
him to find continually ways to keep the servant involved in his needs.
But the master is incapable of dread.

The solution of the servant is work *(Arbeit).* The servant's reality is
self-defined in the activity of his work. The experience of dread has shown
him that he is beyond the master. He must now be cunning toward the
master and pursue his work. "Through work, however, the servant becomes
conscious of what he truly is" (Miller, 195). The solution of the servant
to the problem of his own reality is in his own hands. He has risked his
selfhood in his struggle with the master. At the point where he might have
aspired to become the master, he realized the nothingness and unreality of
the master's position and saw the mode of survival in work.

Another way to put this is that the philosophical mentality almost entered politics but saw the unreality of the state and pulled back into an apparent servitude to the state. The philosophical attitude is born in the mind of the servant. The mentality of the state works for its own ends while the cunning of reason survives in the guise of its apparent servant. The mind of the master sees only at odd moments how strange a partner it has in the philosophical servant who knows the secret of his own work.

Throughout Hegel's system, including the *Philosophy of Right,* Hegel makes clear that the state is not the final master to the philosopher. The philosopher lives under the power of the state, but his work is directed to realities that run counter to it. Philosophy, unlike politics, teaches that world history and absolute spirit are beyond the state. The Master-Servant is a protean form that can take on many contents. One of these is the philosopher's relation to the mastery of the state (or any administrative substructure of power). That Hegel offers here a portrait of philosophical praxis has been missed by traditional commentaries. In this way we can see why what emerges from the Master-Servant are two stages of *philosophical* life: Stoicism and Scepticism. Once Stoicism and Scepticism are understood we can reflect back more fully on the meaning of the Master-Servant as a stage of philosophical existence.

Six

The Unhappy Consciousness

There is a baroque dimension to Hegel's thought, what can be called a baroque line such as is found in baroque arts. To use Heinrich Wöfflin's terms, it is "recessional" in composition and "a-planimetric." The ear or eye follows a major line through each curve or change coming back upon itself and then extending its recession farther until its end in a final recessive curve. The "eye [for Hegel we might say the mind] is continually forced to form recessional relations." [1] The line plays itself out to its end point, but we are ready to enter the totality again. The baroque sense of the recession and the romantic sense of organic wholeness combine in Hegel's sense of dialectic.

In the unhappy consciousness *(unglückliches Bewusstsein)* the line of the *I* plays itself out to a final position from which the whole can be re-entered as Reason. The *I* exhausts its power of formation and can no longer sustain itself as freedom by directly drawing on its powers as *I*. It has discovered the "truth of self-certainty," namely, that the self requires an other and therefore can command no certainty by being itself. The truth about self-certainty is that it is not the truth. But it is in the phenomenon of self-certainty that the nature of truth per se first appears. The stage of Consciousness is dominated by certainty, not truth, because the object is fundamentally experienced as *there* and not as a *there* for consciousness. When consciousness takes up its existence as self, it takes up the existence of the object as there for it. Truth enters because this is the first, the primordial willful step at grasping the two moments of the *Ansich* as corresponding *(entsprechend)*.

The standard way to read the dialectical movement of the *B* section of "The Truth of Self-Certainty" is to associate Stoicism and Scepticism with those forms of these doctrines found in ancient Greece and Rome and to associate the "unhappy consciousness" with the religious life of the European Middle Ages. Hegel himself encourages this and it is surely right to see

70

these historical events as involved in Hegel's meaning. In describing Stoicism he refers to it as being "on the throne or in chains" (Miller, 199), his reference being Marcus Aurelius, Stoic emperor of Rome and Epictetus, Stoic slave freed after the death of Nero. Hegel's reference in regard to Scepticism is most likely to Pyrrhonism and the codifier of Greek scepticism, Sextus Empiricus. Certainly Sextus and the school of scepticism he represents refused to paralyze everyday life with doubt. This position fits Hegel's statement about scepticism that: "It affirms the nullity of seeing, hearing, etc., yet it is itself seeing, hearing, etc. It affirms the nullity of ethical principles, and lets its conduct be governed by these very principles" (Miller, 205). When we recall that the motivation behind this scepticism was to attain *ataraxia,* a state of unperturbedness, we can immediately see how scepticism fits as a successor stage of consciousness to the stoicial.[2] Historically, Sextus Empiricus, who lived about 250 A.D., is later than Marcus Aurelius or Epictetus.

These figures are historical matches to Hegel's two periods. There is a correspondence between medieval religion and unhappy consciousness. The section on unhappy consciousness is interpreted as corresponding to Hegel's discussion of the feudal world and the church crusades in his *Lectures on the Philosophy of History.* It is usually said in this connection that since there is no given term for this medieval life of the self comparable to Stoicism or Scepticism, Hegel simply offers the term, *unglückliches Bewusstsein.* Here the self places the other of itself in a realm absolutely distant from itself such that the priest is required as mediator, as middle term between *unwandelbares Bewusstsein* and *unwesentliches Bewusstsein.* This middle term, Hegel says, is *ein bewusstes Wesen* (Hoffmeister, p. 169; see Miller, 227). Consciousness occupies three places at once.

Hegel's references to elements of medieval Christian faith run throughout this section, as Baillie has noted in footnotes to his English translation (Baillie, pp. 253–67). Hegel's reference to consciousness finding its reality in the grave *(Grab)* (Miller, 217) is amplified when seen in relation to his comments on the Crusades in his *Philosophy of History.* Hegel says: "Whole shiploads of earth were brought from the Holy Land to Europe. Of Christ himself no corporeal relics could be obtained, for he was arisen: the Sacred Handkerchief, the Cross, and lastly the Sepulchre, were the most venerated memorials. But in the Grave is found the real point of retroversion. . . . Christendom was not to find its ultimatum of truth in the grave. . . . We have seen how the vast idea of the union of the Finite with the Infinite was perverted to such a degree as that men looked for a *definite embodiment* of the Infinite in a mere isolated outward object (the Host). Christendom found the empty Sepulchre, but not the union of the Secular and the Eternal; and so it lost the Holy Land."[3] Hegel's remark on a "musical thinking" that is no more than the "chaotic jingling of bells, or a mist of warm incense" (Miller, 217) and his reference to consciousness as doing what is foreign to it, "a thinking and speaking of what is meaningless to it" (Miller, 228) are ironic statements on the church mass, the Latin rather than the vernacular mass.

There can be little doubt but that Hegel meant to connect this stage of unhappy consciousness with medieval Christianity in the way that he connects the previous two stages with Greek and Roman thought. But why did he call it the unhappy consciousness? Why such a metaphorical name? Why not call these stages of the self Stoicism, Scepticism, and Religiosity (to distinguish it from the sense of religion that he wishes to discuss later)? Why not use some term parallel to the other two and one that directly conveys the reference to the religious? In fact at this point one begins to wonder what the significance of the relation of these stages of consciousness to their historical periods really is. How useful is it to make these historical references the basis of our understanding them? For example, John Findlay remarks, in connection with Hegel's characterization of thought as the ringing of bells and the spread of incense: "Surely a strange characterization of the age that produced Aquinas." [4] And of Hegel's passage on monkish asceticism, in which Hegel concludes: "we have here only a personality confined to its own self and its own petty actions, a personality brooding over itself, as wretched as it is impoverished" (Miller, 225), Findlay remarks: "Again a strange distortion of a mode of life which must often have been orderly and happy." [5] Yet Findlay interprets these stages in terms of their historical content, as does, for example, Hyppolite.

The term "unhappy consciousness" in English comes quite close to the term Hegel is using, *unglückliches Bewusstsein,* but it is somewhat misleading. "Unhappy" in its early English meaning has similar connotation to *unglücklich,* that is, not fortunate, unlucky. But the present connotation of unlucky involves the sense of not cheerful or glad, a sense of psychological state that is a passing state. It connotes that the individual can be cheered up, made to feel better about things, look at the bright side. It has the sense of *froh* or *fröhlich*—glad, joyful, gay, happy, cheerful, merry, joyous— or its opposite, being *nicht froh.* Hegel's term is tied to *Glück*—luck, fortune, good luck, success, prosperity, happiness, fate, chance. Or, more specifically, to its opposite, *Unglück*—misfortune, ill luck, distress, misery, affliction, woe, accident, calamity, catastrophe. The *unglückliche Bewusstsein* is an unlucky, hapless, ill-fated, ill-starred consciousness—a consciousness that is *in misfortune.* The term *unglücklich* captures the sense that consciousness in this state has come into it through some set of objective conditions, some definite and perhaps fated path that depends little on the notion of its psychological state of cheerfulness or lack of it.

To speak generally, the stages of consciousness in the *Phenomenology* are not arrived at by an inductive generalization of the characteristics of historical periods. No study of history will allow one to arrive at the order of forms of the *Phenomenology.* The *Phenomenology* is a science of the experience of consciousness, and this means that these stages develop and form themselves in a necessary sequence based on the sense of necessity present in the bond of the double *Ansich* that I have discussed previously. The *Phenomenology* develops independently of history because it is the real order of appearance. It is the hidden structure of all appearance and the course of consciousness in its surpassing of appearance in the achievement of absolute knowing. Thus we can employ the *Phenomenology* or any one of its stages to interpret history or any epoch or stance of human activity toward the object in history. But we cannot truly employ history or some portion of historical experience as the basis to interpret the *Phenomenology*. There is an asymmetrical relation between history and phenomenology. History is a contingent order of events. Phenomenology is a necessary order. The philosophy of history is an application of phenomenological order to the interpretation of the contingency of history.

To apply this point to the matter at hand, the stage of Stoicism in the *Phenomenology* tells us something about Stoicism as a historical phenomenon, about, for example, the Later Stoa that involves the thought of Marcus Aurelius and Epictetus. But the Stoicism of this period of Roman thought and *Geist* does not offer us anything fundamental in terms of interpreting the stage of consciousness called Stoicism—that which by dialectical necessity develops between Masterhood and Servitude and Scepticism. The Stoicism of history offers us a kind of image, a *Bild* of what Hegel is talking about. Stoicism is a real standpoint of self-consciousness that can be found many different places in contingent experience: among the bodyguard of Nero and on the throne of Rome. Unless this relationship of phenomenology to history in Hegel's thought is kept in mind, it is easy to be misled. Although there are fleeting connections made by Hegel between his description of these stages and historical material from the ancient and medieval worlds, we can hardly conclude that his presentation of the freedom of self-consciousness is in essence a description of the transition from the ancient to the medieval periods. But from these periods we can draw valuable images to envision what kind of self-consciousness Hegel is talking about, as we can at other points in the *Phenomenology*, e.g., between the section on Enlightenment and the Enlightenment and between Absolute Freedom and Terror and the French Revolution.

In discussing the section on Masterhood and Servitude, I emphasized its importance as the form of the relation of philosophical activity to the state. There are many other contexts in which the Master-Servant metaphor can be understood—economic, political, psychological—but it also can be understood as presenting a rudimentary standpoint that consciousness must attain in order to begin philosophical thought. At the end of this section the master does not disappear, for nothing fundamental disappears in the course of consciousness, but the servant has come to know the unreality of the master's being and has learned this through his own apprehension of the unreality or nothingness of the object through work. There are several reasons to recommend reading the Master-Servant as the primordial structure of philosophical life.

(1) When consciousness as self-consciousness emerges on the side of the servant from the master-servant struggle, it immediately assumes a philosophical position, that of Stoicism. (2) Hegel introduces Stoicism as *thinking* (Miller, 197). The work that Stoicism takes up in order to have its freedom of the self is thinking. The work of the servant must have involved thinking in some sense. It must not have been simple *Arbeit* but must have also involved a mental dimension, *Gedankenarbeit*.[6] In fact, in introducing Stoicism Hegel says that this thinking was a kind of imaging, a pictorial thinking. This kind of thinking is contrasted with that of Stoicism, which has a primordial form of genuine conceptual thinking. Hegel says: "Thinking moves about the object not in mental images *[Vorstellungen]* or concrete forms *[Gestalten]*, but in concepts *[Begriffen]*" (Hoffmeister, p. 152; Miller, 197). Thus what immediately emerges from the Master-Servant section is the thought of the concept, the work of philosophy itself. (3) That which emerges from the whole section on the self-consciousness and in particular from the freedom of self-consciousness is described by Hegel as a philosophical position, namely *idealism*. Hegel begins his description of "The Certainty and Truth of Reason" with idealism. Thus a very strong reason for seeing the Master-Servant as the primordial structure of philosophical life is that what directly emerges from it is a version of the philosophical. The whole section on the freedom of self-consciousness takes us on to the philosophical position that Hegel calls idealism that begins Reason.

There is much here that the philosopher can learn about his own art and its grounding in the self. Here Hegel is giving his own account of the ancient Socratic project of self-knowledge. The *Phenomenology* is a very special teaching in the emergence of the philosophical standpoint of spirit. In the stage of Consciousness (A.) Hegel has shown us what the philosophical consciousness is not. It is not knowledge without the self, simple knowledge of the world. It is knowledge in which the self is directed to the self without seeing the self as an object simply separate from the world. Thus, as Hegel describes this in introducing Stoicism: "For what is called *thinking* is not the *abstract I*, but the I, which has at the same time the meaning of being *in-itself*, being the object itself, or being objective reality, having the meaning of *being-for-itself* of consciousness, that for which the reality is" (Hoffmeister, pp. 151–52, my trans.; see Miller, 197). The dialectic that Hegel has established between Consciousness (A.) and Self-consciousness (B.) is between the mind wishing just to think the world and it wishing to achieve self-knowledge. Philosophical consciousness per se is born in self-consciousness. But the philosophical mind once born will forget and continue to desire to think the world as something in itself.

As I have discussed, on the final page of the *Phenomenology* Hegel connects the philosophical mind of the *Phenomenology* with recollection *(Erinnerung)*. Philosophy is a kind of memory, of not forgetting. When we forget we return to the world. We think in a present and when we do this, no self-knowing is possible. We lose the self and fail to remember our experience of the nothingness of the object, an experience that was won in a life and death struggle. We risk becoming merely a *person* again and not a philosopher. The connection of philosophy with *Erinnerung* is made clear by Hegel in introducing the "Certainty and Truth of Reason." Hegel says: "Reason is the certainty of consciousness that it is all reality; thus does idealism express its concept" (Miller, 233). Hegel does not mean by idealism here his own idealism. He means a state of mind wherein the knower has a confidence that the object is in some sense mind, that the object is under my power as thinker. Thought or reason is the way in which objects can be made mine. The first way in which this is manifest is as "observational reason."

This first appearance of reason is a return to an interest in the world. The project of self-knowledge begun in the freedom of self-consciousness is lost or just assumed and the original interest of Consciousness (A.) is taken up now with a new sense of mineness. The mine that was lost to the universal in the inversion of language in *Das Meinen* is now regained in a new stance. Hegel explains this new immediacy, the immediacy of reason, especially observational reason, in terms of the phenomenon of *forgetting*. Consciousness forgets the path it has traveled. It forgets its primordial grasp of the project of self-knowledge. As simple self-consciousness (B.) it has not learned fully the philosophical art, the art of recollection. Hegel says: "The consciousness which is this truth has this path behind it and has forgotten *[vergessen]* it, and comes on the scene *immediately* as Reason; in other words, this Reason which comes immediately on the scene appears only as the *certainty* of that truth. Thus it merely *asserts* that it is all reality, but does not itself comprehend this; for it is along that forgotten path *[jener vegessene Weg]* that this immediately expressed assertion is comprehended" (Miller, 233).

What consciousness is trying to do is to learn to recollect, to remember itself in systematic form. But it forgets. Reason comes on the scene by an act of forgetting, of *Vergesslichkeit,* of forgetfulness or negligence. This stage of reason is that of the scientific observation of nature and mind, the activity in which the world is made mine. Its fatal flaw is that it is not founded on the philosophical act of recollection but on its opposite, the act of forgetting. Science is a kind of forgetting, a living in the present. It begins in a forgetting of the way and it will work itself out in an elaborate baroque line to an end in Spirit itself. Scientific *Wissenschaft* is the act of forgetting the self. Philosophical *Wissenschaft* is the act of recollecting it. The scientist forgets himself in the world and presupposes the mine (only in the end to try to observe it, i.e., Observational Reason, sections b. and c.) and thus has no science of his science. In calling his philosophy science *(Wissenschaft)* Hegel steals the club of Hercules, the very term of science's identity, the term whereby the scientist calls the world mine. The way in which Hegel accomplishes this cunning theft is by recollection.

Hegel remembers that science is not born from the head of Zeus, but comes from the self, which itself comes from consciousness of the object. Thus Hegel outwits science by the science of the experience of consciousness and assigns science its cabins in his *Narrenschiff.* Like every stage of consciousness in the *Phenomenology* Reason pretends really to know. But reason turns out to be foolish in the end, a partial knowing, based on an ignorance of the whole that is the true. At the moment of its arrival in spirit reason forgets its own path of birth, and so its ground remains unstable. As the observers of this process we are saved from Reason as a stage in the science of the experience of consciousness by remembering the lost project of self-knowing. Recollection is the remedy of folly (partial thinking) and the positive moment of learned ignorance.

Scientific reason has failed to learn Nicholas of Cusa's truth that: "Nothing could be more beneficial for even the most zealous searcher for knowledge than his being in fact most learned in that very ignorance which is peculiarly his own." [7] Scientific reason fails to learn its ignorance of the self, its presupposition of the mine. Philosophy learns this ignorance and achieves a more efficacious science than science. Nicholas's two principles by which he founds modern philosophy are at work in Hegel's *Phenomenology*—the absolute and learned ignorance (this is not to mention the *coincidentia oppositorum* which is also there). Nicholas begins the philosophy of the absolute with his conception of the *absolutum maximum.* [8] At Hegel's hands philosophy learns the ignorance of consciousness, its follies, by recollection of them. It achieves its freedom from ignorance by remembering the true is the whole. Philosophy learns that its own kind of ignorance is forgetting. Neglect of the whole damages the project of the self-knowledge of the whole. The philosophical element in consciousness must continually correct consciousness itself, which always will fall back toward the outward sense of the object that was its first experience as sense certainty. As Hegel says in that stage: "That is why the natural consciousness, too, is always reaching this result, learning from experience what is true in it; *but equally it is always forgetting it and starting the movement all over again*" (Miller, 109, emphasis mine).

With these points in mind about the essentially philosophical nature of the section on Self-Consciousness and the way that Reason makes its beginning through forgetfulness, I wish to turn to some specific remarks about the interpretation of the unhappy consciousness.

Of Stoicism Hegel says: "As a universal form of the World-Spirit, Stoicism could only appear on the scene in a time of universal fear and bondage, but also a time of universal culture which had raised itself to the level of thought" (Miller, 199). In so stating Hegel makes clear the connection between the Master-Servitude structure and Stoicism. He says further, concerning Scepticism: "It is clear that just as Stoicism corresponds to the *concept* of the *independent* consciousness which appeared as the master and servant relationship, so Scepticism corresponds to its *realization* as a negative attitude towards otherness, to desire and work" (Miller, 202). Stoicism and Scepticism are each ways of responding to the duality established in the Master-Servant. Scepticism seeks *ataraxia* but instead falls into a trivial version of the inverted world, a simple saying of yes and no. Thus Hegel says of Scepticism: "Point out likeness or identity to it, and it will point out unlikeness or non-identity; and when it is now confronted with what it has just asserted, it turns round and points out likeness or identity. Its talk is in fact like the squabbling of self-willed children, one of whom says *A* if the other says *B*, and in turn says *B* if the other says *A*, who by contradicting *themselves* buy for themselves the pleasure of continually contradicting *one another*" (Miller, 205). Inversion here is not a nightmare of not knowing what defines reality, such that we cry out "What if *we* were fiction too?"—but a simple game in which the reality of the self as audience has been won, and it can change to their opposite the fictive meanings of the play. As Hegel says, the sceptic affirms the nothingness of seeing and hearing but sees and hears (Miller, 205).

Hegel says the unhappy consciousness is "one which *knows* that it is the dual consciousness of itself . . . the *Unhappy Consciousness* is the consciousness of self as a dual-natured, merely contradictory being" (Miller, 206). Through Stoicism and Scepticism consciousness has mastered the role it must play in relation to external mastery. The philosopher has learned to live in the state. He has the cunning to continue the work of philosophical thought while bowing correctly to the master. With this mastered, the mastery of its own self becomes the problem. Philosophy takes on a kind of faith in itself. Indeed its thought assumes the form of faith, a thought of faith. Findlay says: "Much of what Hegel here says would assort better with Kierkegaard's morbid Protestant Christianity than with the positive, often joyous attitude of Mediaeval Christendom."[9] Findlay's comment suggests what I have tried to show earlier, that the stage of unhappy consciousness is a philosophical standpoint of mind. It is one that has a connection with medieval thought as well as with Kierkegaard and thus with others. It is not a portrayal of the total medieval form of spirit.

Consciousness falls onto ill-luck, misfortune. The primordial philosophical grasp of things strikes onto the concept of the absolute but apprehends it as the "unchangeable," *Unwandelbarkeit*. Hegel says: "Here, then, we have a struggle against an enemy, to vanquish whom is really to suffer defeat, where victory in one consciousness is really lost in its opposite" (Miller, 209). Philosophy has learned to master the other as another self that dominates its conditions of life but it now must master itself. It attempts to achieve the mastery of the absolute but turns this into the experience of an absolute other. It experiences something similar to what Hegel describes in the *Logic* as the "bad infinity," *schlechte Unendlichkeit.*[10] This unchangeable infinity is that which is ultimately distant from the individual self, like the God of the Middle Ages which Nicholas of Cusa transforms into the *absolutum maximum* or the division between God and the self that Kierkegaard opposes to the thought of "the System." Kierkegaard's thought shows that philosophy can fall into the misfortune of the bad infinity even after the Hegelian pathway has been shown, as well as before. But Kierkegaard's and Hegel's philosophy have much in common, as do any two opposites. They have more in common than most Kierkegaardians or Hegelians would choose to believe.

In the unhappy consciousness the absolute is turned into a beyond *(Jenseits).* In so doing it is misfortune; it experiences an *Unglück.* It is not merely unhappy, for it cannot simply change its attitude toward this other and overcome its lack of mastery. Consciousness as self-consciousness has mastered the Stoical and Sceptical attitudes of thought. It has thought its way through them, but now it becomes unable to think. This consciousness first relates to this other through the heart, then through external action and enjoyment, and finally it humbles itself and becomes wretched (Miller, 223 and 226). It obtains relief from its misery by assigning the necessary feeling, thought, and action in relation to an intermediate other self. This intermediate self is not a synthesis, but evidence of the breakdown of the self's certainty of itself. Self-knowledge has been given up as a project when it is put in the hands of another. This is not a life and death struggle, as the self has already undergone in the Master-Servant; it is a misfortune. But the self in its wretchedness is very close to asking only to be a *person* (Miller, 187), just to be allowed to live in servitude to this other of itself.

At the penultimate moment of despair and misfortune this consciousness remembers the truth it learned in the crucible of the *verkehrte Welt.* It sees the possibility of the *mine,* of the *I,* again. This takes the form of the "idealism" of reason—the observation of the world as mine. Hegel says: "But it lets the mediating agent *[Diener]* express this still ruptured certainty, so that it is only being *in itself [an sich],* its misfortune turned upside down *[sein Unglück das verkehrte],* namely that it is only in its action itself as self-satisfying action, or blessed enjoyment, that its pitiable action is just so *in itself [an sich]* the topsy-turvy *[das Verkehrte],* namely absolute action; the concept in accordance with action is only really action as action of the individual" (Hoffmeister, p. 171; N.B. both Miller, 230 and Baillie, p. 267 confuse the meaning of this passage). The sense of reversal and the reality in the midst of this reversal that consciousness learned in the section on *verkehrte Welt* allows consciousness as self-consciousness generally to see its own single reality in the extremes and middle term of this syllogism. Consciousness, Hegel says, realizes that in its particular individuality there is all reality. This individuality is the immediate version of reason *(Vernunft)*.

Philosophy now gives up its sense of the absolute to exercise its own power to be specific about the things of the world. In so doing it is freed of its misfortune, its *Unglück*. But it also forgets the project of self-knowledge that it began in its freedom as self-consciousness, a project that it will have to bring forward as *Geist* at the end of its long night of reason. It will have to re-evolve its sense of the self while trying to observe mind.

The transition to Reason here is really no transition in the sense of Reason being a "deduction" from the stage of Self-consciousness. There is no inference here in which the one stage is inferred from the other. One is in no way "deduced out" from the other, anymore than is the in-itself as something for consciousness inferred or deduced out from the in-itself as immediately apprehended by consciousness. Yet there is a bond of necessity between these two moments and there is a bond of necessity between Reason and Self-consciousness. The two senses or levels of *Ansich* are the primordial structure of conceptual memory. At the end of Self-consciousness, the self in its unhappy state draws itself forth until it remembers the fact of its own presence. This is simply an ingenious act on the part of self-consciousness—it remembers the experience of world reversal at the end of Consciousness.

This *déjà vu* shows this self the way to a new sense of the mine. And once again consciousness is in possession of the *Ansich.* We as the philosophical observers of this ingenious act of self-consciousness learn something about what happens to philosophy when it becomes unlucky and is stuck in a certain standpoint of mind. It finds itself in this position because it has forgotten some part of the whole. It has forgotten some part of its primordial self and it must go back and remember it. Only then will it find its way out of its difficulties. The most dangerous thing is for philosophy to forget memory. Hegel's whole *Phenomenology* is an attempt to keep us from this loss so that thinking *(Wissen)* can attain its own form and give up its life as the indefinite unseen in the appearance. To show us this very idea Hegel creates his powerful image of misfortune—the philosophical spirit's primordial attempt at the thought of the concept as something absolute. It is more misfortune than tragedy, as tragedy is what surrounds the whole thought of the *Phenomenology.*

Seven

Phrenology

Hegel's section on Phrenology is surely the most curious in the *Phenomenology,* especially for the present-day reader, encountering the work in a time when phrenology and physiognomy are not regarded as serious intellectual pursuits. Or have these pursuits disappeared? Perhaps they have taken on different forms. The standard way to approach this section is to regard Hegel as refuting these pseudo-sciences, as being drawn into a debate with them simply because he recognized them as false. Findlay takes this approach; he says: "Hegel now takes the opportunity to comment scathingly and at length on two pretentious pseudo-sciences of his time, the 'physiognomy' which had been given currency by Lavater, and the much-trumpeted 'phrenology' of Gall." [1] Hegel supposedly takes this opportunity to set the record straight. More systematically it might be argued that Hegel's purpose is to take into account all standpoints of mind, and since physiognomy and phrenology are such standpoints, Hegel must include them. To do otherwise would be to exclude arbitrarily a form of consciousness from the science of the experience of consciousness.

If Hegel just takes the opportunity to refute these popular sciences for the good of the public and the community of scholars generally, why does he do it here? Why not present these views in a separate essay? Why interrupt the project at hand? If Hegel is not interested simply in the refutation of these sciences of mind, but thinks in the interest of completeness that he must include them, why do so at such length and so vividly? Findlay's approach preserves the sense that this section has the air of a digression. Hegel must have been enjoying himself writing these pages. He must have been drinking deep of the wine of the bacchanalian revel as he worked out his digression. As we know from Plato, digressions are often where the most important things are said. Digressions have a long and honorable history in philosophy. Perhaps Hegel included this discussion in the *Phenomenology* not because of a simple principle of completeness, but because he intended to say something about phenomenological science itself in this discussion.

Whenever in reading a great work of philosophy we find a curious passage, and commentators accounting for it by off-hand explanations (offering commonsensical or external historical explanations in terms of the thought or events of the time) instead of philosophical explanations in terms of the text, we should awake and fix our attention. It may be that such a digression or curious passage contains an ironically stated version of the philosopher's position. I believe this is the case with Hegel's discussion of phrenology. I do not know whether Hegel in fact intended this. But in order to understand such a section it may be necessary to interpret it with all the ironic powers the reader can muster.

Although most commentators ignore Hegel's arguments against phrenology, and by tradition most teachers of seminars on Hegel's *Phenomenology* pass over this section with a few remarks on its oddness, its significance as a critique of modern psychology and philosophy of mind has not been missed by some commentators. Hyppolite treats this section quite blandly. Loewenberg, Lauer, and MacIntyre recognize its implications for contemporary theories of mind. Alasdair MacIntyre's "Hegel on Faces and Skulls" is to my knowledge the only essay written especially on this section.[2] MacIntyre says that buried in phrenology is the thesis that biochemical or neural states are sufficient causes of human actions. "This thesis," MacIntyre says, "wore phrenological clothing in 1807; today its clothing is as fashionable as it was then, only the fashions are not what they were." [3] To this can be added Judith Shklar's comment about the social dimension of such "science." Shklar observer: "This 'science' was generally accepted by the most advanced opinion for decades after Hegel wrote. This was no straw man. One need only recall the influence of Cesare Lombroso on criminology to recognize how important a part measuring skulls played in the development of the social sciences. It was Lombroso's belief that by measuring the skulls of prisoners one would determine who was, and by implication who was not, a criminal type. Traces of this sort of reasoning are, in fact, by no means extinct now." [4]

I wish to treat this section on Physiognomy and Phrenology in two ways: (1) I wish to explore the section generally, in terms of its implications for psychology and philosophy of mind; and (2) I wish to treat its general significance for Hegel's *Phenomenology,* to bring out the general ironic point that is hidden in it.

(1) In its stage as Observational Reason, consciousness has passed from the empirical study of nature to the observation of mind. It comes finally, just before the stage of physiognomy and phrenology, to observational psychology, which Hegel says tries to record all sorts of "faculties, inclinations, and passions," and in an act of recalling that the mind as self-consciousness is a unity, it lumps these all together in a bag. It puts them

"together in the mind like things in a bag" (Miller, 303). This form of psychology attempts to look for laws to connect these elements of the mind to the environment. Hegel denies that we can draw a line of difference between the individual on which the environment acts and the individual that is acted upon: "the spherical surface, the world of the individual, has at once an ambiguous meaning" (Miller, 307). Had empirical psychologists read and understood these few pages it would have saved them a great deal of time in the historical development of psychology. Since some psychologists still think this way today, it would continue to save time. What Hegel has shown is not that there is a great deal of difficulty in working out the difference between the individual and the environment of the individual, but that the distinction is in principle faulty. Any causal relationship drawn between the individual and its environment will involve this confusion.

The inability to establish this connection between inner (as the self-consciousness of the individual) and outer (as its *milieu*) leads to the attempt to establish an inner-outer connection in the entity of the individual itself. This takes us to the threshold of physiognomy. Hegel specifically has in mind here the theories of Johann Caspar Lavater (1741–1801) that were a source for Franz Joseph Gall's (1758–1828) science of "phrenology" (although Gall objected to having his science associated with Lavater and his followers). Lavater's claim was that the character and disposition of the individual could be judged from the facial features and form of the body. It was a theory of understanding the character of the individual on the basis of his lineaments. It was, as Hegel says, a kind of geography of the body (Miller, 311). The character of a given individual is evident in the particular geography of his body. The physiognomical scientist is trained to read these signs. The inner is expressed in the outer.

Lavater, in his major work, the *Physiognomische Fragmente* (4 vols., 1775–78), says: "The Science to which I devote my attention is universally diffused, is level to every capacity, is the lot and the inheritance of every Man, and I simply give an account of my own sensations, my observations, and my conclusions. Let it always be recollected, that the external characters are designed to unfold the internal; that every species of human knowledge must quickly cease, if we should lose the faculty of judging of the interior from the exterior." [5] Lavater's work ends with an engraving and description of Descartes and a conclusion of what a great and universal genius he was. Graeme Tytler, in his excellent study, *Physiognomy in the European Novel,* says that when the first volume of Lavater's work appeared it was discussed in practically every European periodical: "For the literary world, the publication of the *Fragmente* was a supreme event." [6] Wieland, in a review, called it "ein klassisches Werk unserer Sprache (a German classic);" [7] Herder reviewed the first volume with great enthusiasm, but the second "so filled Herder with inspiration that he wanted to prostrate himself with joy and 'Gott in jedem Menschen umarmen' (to embrace God in every human being)." [8] Lavater's connections with the best minds of his age included a long correspondence and friendship with Goethe that began in 1773.

This science of lineaments is behavioral psychology. Were Hegel writing today he might just as well here refer to B. F. Skinner. Hegel says: "The speaking mouth, the working hand, and, if you like, the legs too are the organs of performance and actualization which have within them the action *qua* action, or the inner as such" (Miller, 312). The difference between Skinner and Lavater or, later, Gall is that Skinner has done away with the inner entirely. The thesis of Skinner's popular book, *Beyond Freedom and Dignity,* is that freedom and dignity are not secret, inner motivations of individuals, but elements of behavior capable of observation. Like Skinner's thesis, Lavater's and Gall's also have a practical dimension. We can predict or divine behavior, and it follows that if we can do this we can alter behavior and character or in some way come to terms with it. Skinner says: "What is needed is a technology of behavior. . . . One difficulty is that almost all of what is called behavioral science continues to trace behavior to states of mind, feelings, traits of character, human nature, and so on." [9] In this science of lineaments (Skinner's or Lavater's) the inner must ultimately disappear in its expressions in the body. Hegel says: "For that reason we can say with equal truth that these expressions express the inner too much, as that they do so too little: too much because the inner self breaks out in them and there remains no antithesis between them and it" (Miller, 312). We should not be surprised to discover that Skinner has collapsed the inner and the outer.

One is reminded of the joke in which two behaviorists meet on a street corner. One says: "You're ok. How am I?"

One might be tempted to say that there must be some difference between Skinner and such exponents of pseudo-science. Skinner is a controversial but respected figure in the profession of psychology. This is to forget that both Lavater and Gall were quite famous. Gall was a favorite of European aristocracy. Metternich, the Austrian prince and statesman, thought him the greatest mind he had ever known; after his death Gall was mourned as a great pioneer scientist. [10] Why would a science of lineaments be so attractive? Why is it so easily accepted? What accounts for the fact that this attitude of consciousness keeps coming back to us under various names, and will continue to do so, since it is a fundamental way in which consciousness relates to itself?

Hegel's answer is that it is grounded in a sense of the individual's character that serves us every day in our intercourse with others. He says: "We see from a man's face whether he is *in earnest* about what he is saying or doing" (Miller, 318). But the science of physiognomy, Hegel says, overlooks the power of the mask (ibid.). Skinner has overlooked this, too (of course he believes nothing can hide from the searchlight of scientific experimentation, consciously or unconsciously). The face may just as well be understood as a mask in which the inner self is just the opposite in its disposition than as it outwardly appears. What can Skinner tell us of the psychopath who always wears the mask of sanity? With the question of the face as mask this science encounters the principle of the topsy-turvy world that consciousness experienced in its first attempt at understanding the object, at the end of the section on Consciousness (A.). There consciousness faced the problem in terms of the inner and the outer of the object. Here it faces it in terms of the inner and outer of the subject. Hegel says: "Observation accepts this antithesis in the same inverted relationship which characterizes it in the sphere of appearance" (Miller, 319)—"Das Beobachten nimmt diesen Gegensatz nach demselben *verkehrten* Verhältnisse auf, worin er sich in der *Erscheinung* bestimmt" (Hoffmeister, p. 234, emphasis mine).

The philosophical truth of inversion is not necessarily an easy truth to learn. In the early 1960s a report appeared in the *St. Louis Post-Dispatch* of two detectives of the Chattanooga, Tennessee police force who, while investigating the robbery of a pet store in that city, learned that a talking bird for sale in the store had been left uncovered in its cage throughout the night and had witnessed the robbery. It was reported that the detectives questioned the bird for two hours but failed to learn the description of the thieves. These officers of the law were natural physiognomists-behaviorists. They reasoned that since the bird could speak, could anatomically produce the sound of human words, it could also be expected, in some way, to offer a clue to the robbers. But in this case they encountered an organism that was truly all outer, with only an empty parrot's inner, and thus they got from the parrot just what they saw and heard.

Hegel says there is no "science of knowing men" (Miller, 320). This is because there are no laws of character possible. The reading of the signs of behavior or deeds of the individual or the features of his face are merely opinions. In this connection Baillie quotes the interesting line from *Macbeth:* "There is no art to find the mind's construction in the face" (Baillie, p. 347; Act I. 4.). Some men have a talent for reading meanings in the face, but there are no laws of it. It is a kind of genius, and there are no laws of genius, any more than there are laws for the interpretation of aesthetic form.

Laws of human behavior and the prediction of it have no more status than the housewife saying it always rains when she is drying her washing. Such laws have the *meaning of mine.* Hegel takes us back to his original pun on *Meinen* (see Miller, 322; Hoffmeister, pp. 235–36). I believe that I can divine what the person intends or means, his *Meinung,* from his features and deeds, but this *Meinung,* when I state it, is only my *Meinen (meine Meinung),* like the housewife's opinion about the law of rain on washday. As with all prophetic rather than truly predictive statements, I am dealing with a body of completely universal principles and deriving statements about the particular from them that admit of indefinite variation as to their meaning.

Analogously to sense-certainty about the object, I desire to express the meaning of the object as a particular in sense, but end up expressing it only as something that is mine. This sense of it as mine has a completely universal meaning. Like the object of sense which can be seen from an infinite number of perspectives at an infinite number of moments, the individuality being observed is an infinite bundle of possibilities. Hegel says: "In such mere opinion the individuality is infinitely determined and determinable. In the accomplished deed this bad infinity is destroyed" (Miller, 322). Hegel's term here is *schlechte Unendlichkeit* (Hoffmeister, p. 236). This bad infinity of all possibilities residing in the individuality is made truly particular once the individual acts. This reminds one of Hegel's statement of the animals' handling of particularity, of falling to and eating particulars up. Hegel says the proper retort to a physiognomist who claims to have read one's character is to box his ear (Miller, 322). In so doing one has tried not to think character, but to manifest it. Hegel becomes more violent in regard to phrenology's merging of the mind with the skull and says: "the retort here would, strictly speaking, have to go the length of beating in the skull of anyone making such a judgement, in order to demonstrate in a manner just as palpable as his wisdom, that for man, a bone is nothing *in itself,* much less *his* true reality" (Miller, 339).[11] Hegel was not the first to suggest the *argumentum ad baculum* as a genuine philosophical instrument. It goes back to the Pre-Socratics, among whom Diogenes and the Cynics were known to swing their clubs and also to display publicly the organ of generation (about which we will hear shortly from Hegel).[12]

The transition to phrenology from physiognomy is made by the attempt to locate the mind or spirit in an organ. Hegel notes that in common life, as in Plato's *Timaeus,* the liver plays a central role as the seat of the individual (Miller, 326). Hegel is aware that in the traditional arts of divination the liver plays the central role. Thus in moving this center to the nervous system and the brain, phrenology is already creating an abstract sense of the self. Phrenology is concerned with the brain and its presence in the skull. Hegel says that "the brain is the living head, the skull is the *caput mortuum*" (Miller, 328). The skull is the dead head. The skull is not only a dead head; phrenology is a kind of scientific deadheadism. It is a kind of mortuary science of the mind. It examines the mind frozen in its stillness on the surface of the skull, as opposed to examining the mind as something active and self-developing.

To think that the mind is the brain is the first mistake that phrenology makes, and then to interpret the brain through the skull-bone is to compound the error. One is reminded here of Berkeley's argument in the Second

Dialogue between Hylas and Philonous, to show that the mind is not the
brain. Hegel does not make reference to this argument but it is useful here
to bring out Hegel's point.

> *Phil.* I would first know whether I rightly understand your hypothesis.
> You make certain traces in the brain to be the causes or occasions of our
> ideas. Pray tell me whether by the "brain" you mean any sensible thing.
>
> *Hyl.* What else think you I could mean?
>
> *Phil.* Sensible things are all immediately perceivable; and those things
> which are immediately perceivable are ideas, and these exist only in the
> mind. This much you have, if I mistake not, long since agreed to.
>
> *Hyl.* I do not deny it.
>
> *Phil.* The brain therefore you speak of, being a sensible thing, exists only
> in the mind.[13]

There is no more simple answer to all brain-mind theorists—the brain
is a perception in the mind. The brain is an idea (sensible or otherwise)
that the mind forms of itself. In principle the brain cannot be equated
with the mind, because the mind makes the equation. The phrenologist
goes on to attempt to observe mind as the skull. But the problem would
remain even if we did not attempt this geography of the skull. If physiognomy
is really just behaviorism, then phrenology is what in the tradition of Anglo-
American analytic philosophy is called "philosophical psychology."

Philosophical psychology since Ryle's classical work, *The Concept of Mind,*
has been dedicated to the same goal as phrenology, but without the models
of the head, and without examining any actual heads, but instead examining
claims of psychologists. Ryle sets up the program with his theory of the
"ghost in the machine," the theory of an inner and outer world to the
human individual. Ryle says: "The important thing is that the practice of
describing specifically human doings according to the recommended meth-
odology quickly made it apparent to psychologists how shadowy were the
supposed 'inner-life' occurrences which the Behaviourists were at first
reproached for ignoring or denying. . . . The Behaviourists' methodological
programme has been of revolutionary importance to the programme of
psychology." [14] Apparently it has also been to the program of philosophical
psychology. The instinct that philosophical psychology has followed is to
get rid of the notion of mind as "inner." It is this search out and destroy
mission that it carries out against mind as inner that "philosophical psychology" shares with phrenology.

To this point I have tried to emphasize that Hegel is refuting not simply
pseudo-sciences in this section but also those doctrines of psychological
science that attempt to observe mind and those philosophies of mind that

are caught in the inner and outer distinction concerning mind. I do not mean that Hegel is refuting psychology. He is attacking certain forms of psychological investigation for which philosophical claims are made. Hegel is quite willing to give all these their place in his doctrine of appearance. He even seems personally attracted to palmistry and handwriting analysis. Under Hegel's analysis of physiognomy we could also include all contemporary popular doctrines of the mind—"body language," what is reported on in *Psychology Today,* personality quizzes in mass magazines, etc.[15] These are all harmless if we recognize them as simply part of the general furniture of consciousness. But Hegel's treatment of phrenology raises issues of a more general significance for the *Phenomenology* and it is to this, the second of my points, that I wish to turn now.

(2) The last lines of Hegel's judgment on phrenology are some of the most extraordinary in the *Phenomenology.* Hegel is always a forceful critic. But here he uses both ironic and strong language. In both the English translations what Hegel says has been made to sound a bit more "dignified" than what he actually says. The final two sentences of this section are: "The *depth,* that spirit drives out from within, but does so only as far as the level of *pictorial consciousness* and then stays on this level, and the *ignorance* of this consciousness, what it is, what it says, is the same linking of high and low that in the living being nature naïvely expresses in linking the organ of its highest perfection, the organ of procreating, and the organ of pissing. The infinite judgment as infinite is the perfection of its own self-comprehended life; but consciousness of the infinite judgment remaining at the pictorial level retains itself as pissing *[Pissen]*" (Hoffmeister, p. 254, my trans.; Miller, 346).

Phrenological consciousness, that literally sees the brain pictured on the regions of the head, is just pissing off. The phrenologist who uses his own mental powers to understand the nature of mind and in so doing gets no further in its understanding than he does, is like someone who, when confronted with his sex organ, discovers he can piss, and becomes so fascinated with this function that he never sees that this organ is also good for sexual pleasure and the procreative act. In this passage Hegel does not say urination, *Urinieren,* but pissing, *Pissen.* To render this as "urination," as do Baillie and Miller, is to rob us of the force of Hegel's statement. The phrenological understanding of mind is a deeply false grasp of the infinite judgment that is absolute knowing. Phrenology is an ignorance, an unknowing *(Unwissenheit)* masquerading not only as a *Wissenschaft,* but as genuine *Wissen*—the self-knowledge of spirit. Hegel may intend a wordplay on *Pissen* and *Wissen.*

Why does Hegel use such strong language here? To answer that, he is perhaps personally incensed at the pseudo level of science in phrenology, which, no doubt, is to give only a partial answer. In this section Hegel emphasizes the skull, how phrenology has reduced the mind to the skull, e.g., "the disgracefulness of the irrational, crude thought which takes a bone for the reality of self-consciousness" (Miller, 209). The term Hegel uses for phrenology is not *Phrenologie*. Hegel uses *Schädellehre*, literally skull-teaching or skull-doctrine—*craniology*. Gall's theory was first known as craniology. Gall disapproved of and refused to use the term, phrenology.[16] Phrenology, "science of mind," was coined by his disciple and colleague, Johann Georg Spurzheim (1776–1832), who by changing this one essential gave this science the role of a philosophical movement. After his partnership with Gall ended in Paris in 1813, Spurzheim went on to lecture with great success in Britain and America.

Gall began to form his doctrine of *Schädellehre* in the early 1790s. In 1796 Gall began giving lectures in Vienna, but these were stopped after five years by decree of the Austrian government because his lectures were judged dangerous to religion. Nahum Capen, editor of "The Phrenological Library," reports in his "Biography of Dr. Gall" that several books describing his theories were published by Gall students in 1802 and he gives the titles of three of these.[17] Gall's theories spread through Germany and in 1805 Gall and Spurzheim left Vienna to travel and lecture in Germany, Switzerland, and the Low Countries. Between 1805 and 1807, when Gall settled in Paris, they visited most major cities in that part of Europe. The list of cities visited given by Capen includes Jena. Hegel could have heard these lectures. Of these travels Gall states: "The circumstances were too favorable to permit me to resist the invitations which came to me from most of the Universities." [18] Gall's major work, *Anatomie et physiologie du système nerveux en général, et du cerveau en particulier,* appeared in Paris in 1810–19. Hegel must have known of the doctrines of *Schädellehre* from Gall's intense activity prior to his arrival in Paris in 1807, the year Hegel's *Phenomenology* was published.

The point toward which I am working in order to understand Hegel's attack on phrenology can be seen philologically in the contrast between the terms *Schädellehre* and *Schädelstätte*. *Schädelstätte* is Calvary or Golgotha. It is the term Hegel uses at the very end of the *Phenomenology* to describe the nature of the *Phenomenology* itself. He says: "The *goal,* absolute knowing, or spirit knowing itself as spirit has for its path the recollection *[Erinnerung]* of spirits as they are to themselves and accomplish the organization of their realm. Their preservation on the side of their free existence, appearing in the form of contingency, is history, but on the side of their conceptually grasped organization is the *science* of *the coming into appearance of knowing;* both together, conceptually grasped history, form the recollection *[Erinnerung]* and the Calvary of absolute spirit, the reality, truth, and certainty of its throne, without which it would be lifeless solitude; only—from the chalice of this realm of spirits/foams out to Him His infinity" (Hoffmeister, p. 564, my trans.).

Calvary or Golgotha is literally the place of the skull. This literal meaning is preserved in the German word *Schädel-stätte* (*Schädel*, skull; *stätte*, place) as it is not in English, although *calvaria* is the Latin root of Calvary and Golgotha reflects the original Aramaic *gülgülthā*, of which the Latin *calvaria* is the translation. Calvary is the proper name of the Mount on which the Christ was crucified. Figuratively it is an experience of intense mental suffering. Hegel uses the term to describe the process of the *Phenomenology*.

Phenomenology is the "recollection and the Calvary of absolute spirit." The true sense of the skull is found only in phenomenology, not in phrenology. The phenomenological study of consciousness comprehends consciousness in its erotic course of procreation of forms of itself to the point of absolute knowledge where consciousness can recollect its "highway of despair." Phrenology is a false science of the skull. It is logos without eros, mere *Pissen*. The skull in phrenology, as Hegel says, is a *caput mortuum*. It is dead—dead, inert mind. Phenomenology is a logos of eros, of the life of mind, the self-movement of spirit toward the life of absolute knowing. Phrenology sounds like phenomenology. Phrenology is the inverted world, the upside-down version of phenomenology. *Schädelstätte*, as the symbol of the true science of mind, stands to *Schädellehre*, as the false science of mind, as the true erotic act of procreation stands to the perfunctory act of pissing. Phrenology must be attacked so strongly, as an illusion of consciousness in its road to self-knowledge, not simply because it is a pseudo-science and represents bad thinking, but because it is the natural opposite, the inversion of the true science of mind—phenomenology. Phenomenology is a science of the appearance of *Geist* and so is phrenology such a science.

In relation to physiognomy Hegel says the invisibility of spirit is to be made visible; this is how physiognomy differs from psychology. Hegel says: "In physiognomy, on the other hand, Spirit is supposed to be known in its *own* outer aspect, as in a being which is the *utterance* of Spirit—the visible invisibility of its essence" (Miller, 323). This notion of the visible invisibility *(die sichtbare Unsichtbarkeit)* is taken up further when Hegel discusses the sense of an everyday phrenology (Miller, 336). Here Hegel says there is a kind of false sense of possibility achieved through imagination *(Vorstellung)*, not through true thinking. We can imagine the possibility of a bump connected with a trait of character: "But if *possibility* is taken, not in the sense of the possibility of *imagining* but in the sense of *inner* possibility, or the possibility of the *concept*, then the object is a reality of the kind which is a pure 'thing,' and is, and should be, without a significance of this sort, and can, therefore, have it only in imagination or picture-thinking" (Miller, 336). We cannot think mind in terms of such possibilities as phrenology claims, but we can visualize these possibilities because we can visualize any possibilities we wish to, such as "the flying cow, that was first caressed by the crab, that was riding on the donkey, etc. etc." (ibid.).

Like phenomenology, phrenology is a science of the visible invisibility of the mind or spirit. Phenomenology is attempting to bring forth the unseen from the seen, the *Begriff* from the *Bild.* We must be able in the science of phenomenology to see the spirit as *Begriff* as it works its way through appearances. Phrenology is a science that lets us see the invisible spirit easily in the geography of the skull. It is easy because it lets us see anything we want. It is the judgment of bad infinity, the infinity that is endless possibility. The thought of the concept is the true infinity because it is a self-expanding infinite in which only certain things are possible, dependent upon the settled state of affairs of the course taken to that point (see the discussion of bad infinity in the *Logic*). This is why in the last sentence of this section Hegel speaks of the true infinite judgment in contrast to the infinite judgment that remains on the level of imagining *(Vorstellen)*. The infinite on the level of *Vorstellen* is a mental pissing.

I want to come finally to what Hegel says in Miller's paragraph 340. Hegel says: "The crude instinct of self-conscious Reason will reject out of hand such a 'science' of phrenology *[Schädelwissenschaft]*. . . . But the worse the conception, the less sometimes does it occur to one wherein its badness specifically lies, and the harder it is to analyse it." *Schädelwissenschaft* is dangerous because of its simplicity. When thought becomes so false as to be the reverse of true thought, it is difficult to know wherein its badness, its *Schlechtigkeit* lies. Partial truths are more easily grasped as partial than the opposite of truth.

Hegel continues: "But Reason, in its role of observer, having reached thus far, seems also to have reached its peak, at which point it must abandon itself and do a right-about turn; for only what is wholly bad is implicitly charged with the immediate necessity of changing round into its opposite." This last phrase goes: "denn erst das ganz Schlechte hat die unmittelbare Notwendigkeit an sich, sich zu verkehren" ("because only the wholly bad has the immediate necessity in itself to turn itself upside down"). Note Hegel's term here is *verkehren.* The verb in the first part of the sentence is *sich überschlagen,* literally to go head over heels, capsize, turn a somersault. In the last sentence of the paragraph Hegel uses the term *Umkehrung,* overturning, inversion. He says: "Thus it is that this final stage of Reason in its observational role is its worst; and that is why its reversal *[Umkehrung]* becomes a necessity." Then follows a summary of the course of spirit to this point, ending with Hegel's final accusation concerning pissing.

In this passage (340) Hegel is playing on the topsy-turvy world metaphor. The immediate somersault that reason must accomplish is the manifestation of the self through its own activity. But Hegel's statements here have a wider significance. Phrenology is the upside-down of phenomenology. It is science gone bad, not just gone bad as empirical psychology, but gone bad as philosophical science. Phrenology would replace the *Schädelstätte* with the *Schädelstelle*. It would reduce Calvary to a simple bone.

Hegel must make clear the difference between the science of the experience of consciousness and the science of psychology in any of its forms. If this is not done, phenomenology will be seen as a kind of psychological science or as a type of thinking that works with psychology in some fashion, much as the phenomenology of Husserl does today. What psychology does not have is a doctrine of recollection. Psychology, like contemporary descriptive phenomenology, stands immediately before the object and observes it. It is a "pure" science because it cannot comprehend the object in terms of a recollection of its own internal being. The internal perspective, the selfness of consciousness, is there only through recollective memory.

For a science of the experience of consciousness, consciousness in itself must be both inside and outside its object at once. It must be both the *we* and the consciousness undergoing the process of self-movement that is the prime matter of the *Phenomenology*. In the act of recollecting, consciousness is both inside the memory being recalled and outside it as the power of its recall. In phrenology this inner and outer is broken up into a simple static relation of mind to skull. Any knowledge that reason may obtain by recollection is now impossible. It can now only observe and divine. It is in the bad infinite where all possibilities are possible. Only recollection can provide the true infinite as a *phenomenon* because it is a process of building endlessly back into itself. Memory or recollection is not pictorial thought *(Vorstellung)* because its images form a necessary infinite sequence. Ever present in them is the *Begriff*. Phrenological thought is just pictorial thought because it is an infinite of images with no necessary connection between them. It is more correctly just one image, the image of the geographic skull. It is just thought, pissing.

Eight

Two Forms of Defective Selfhood: The Spiritual Animal Kingdom and the Beautiful Soul

One of the most curiously titled and abstractly presented sections in the *Phenomenology* is: "Das geistige Tierreich und der Betrug oder die Sache selbst" ("The Spiritual Animal Kingdom and Humbug, or the Matter in Hand Itself"). It introduces the last stage of reason where individuality believes itself to be real in and for itself. It is a degenerate form of reason and, as the first terms of its title indicate, it is a proto yet false form of *Geist*. It is a kind of animal form of spirit that precedes the introduction of spirit proper, i. e., the sixth chapter of the *Phenomenology*. It is a stage of *Betrügerei,* of cheating, trickery, deceit, fraud, swindling, a kind of final humbuggery of reason enacted just before it gives itself up to the moral concerns of *Geist*. Its object is the *Sache selbst,* the practical thing, the cause, the business to be done, the event, the fact, the goods. What can Hegel mean by this curious metaphorical title? Unlike other metaphorical titles, unlike the *verkehrte Welt* (which is not itself the title of a section) or the *unglückliche Bewusstsein,* this title seems to convey little in itself. When we turn to the presentation of this form of consciousness we find little framework of reference. Hegel discusses it in quite abstract and systematic terms.

I wish to consider this section from two perspectives: (1) I wish to provide a contemporary frame of reference for what Hegel is discussing, and (2) I wish to suggest that Hegel's title for this section can in a certain sense be applied to the project of the *Phenomenology* as a whole. From these points I will move to the notion of the beautiful soul, which has a certain consequential relationship to the life of the *Tierreich*. In selecting these two sections my interest is in the juxtaposition of two senses of selfhood, one at the end of Reason (the spiritual animal kingdom), the other at the end of Spirit (the beautiful soul).

Findlay is very close to the sense of this animal kingdom (which he calls the "spiritual zoo") when he says: "The cult of the Matter-in-hand is, therefore, yet another case of that self-absorbed high-mindedness of which we have had instances in the case of Stoicism, Scepticism, the pursuit of Virtue and the Law of the Heart. Not only was it the typical vice of German Romanticism, but we may identify it also as the vice of the American business executive, the nineteenth-century empire builder, the disinterestedly frightful Nazi, or the pure practitioner of scholarship or research. (This last was probably most in Hegel's mind.) " [1] I believe Findlay is right, that if Hegel has any specific context in mind as an illustration of this stage, it is the world of the pure researcher who wishes to command the world as his, as a *mine* of his advanced self-consciousness.

There is no real community of truth here. Each researcher pretends to be concerned with the common pursuit of truth but is concerned with the work of others only to further his own sense of mind, of the truth that *I* have discovered. The original problem of the *mine* comes back to affect this process since the truth that I discover is not truly mine. As truth it is there for others to see. There is a kind of humbuggery here in two ways. It is humbug to try to own the results of research. And it is humbug to work alone in one's study, like Descartes before the stove with his meditations, with interest in making only my discoveries, placing them alongside those of other gentlemen scholars. This is far from the Socratic speech of the *agora,* in which questions are put in common between individuals and their answers commonly sought, and where no one owns the outcome.

Further, I think Findlay is right in suggesting the connection of this stage with the "nineteenth-century empire builder," "the disinterestedly frightful Nazi," and "the American business executive," as well as the "pure practitioner" of research. Hegel's stages in the *Phenomenology* are fundamental structures of consciousness that appear in various historical forms. What Findlay's images suggest is that the stage of the animal kingdom is what has been called technological consciousness or technological society. When we add up the sequence of the nineteenth-century empire builder, the Nazi, the American business executive, and the pure researcher, we get contemporary technological consciousness. If placing the Nazi within this sequence seems odd, we have only to consider Heidegger's observation in his *Einführung in die Metaphysik (An Introduction to Metaphysics),* delivered first by Heidegger in 1935 at Freiburg and re-published by him in 1953 in a text unchanged in content, but in which he rectified imprecisions. Heidegger says: "In 1928 there appeared the first part of a general bibliography on the concept of value. In it 661 titles are listed. No doubt the number has meanwhile swollen to one thousand. All these works call themselves philosophy. The works that are being peddled about nowadays as the philosophy of National Socialism but have nothing whatever to do with the inner truth and greatness of this movement (namely the encounter between global technology and modern man)—have all been written by men fishing in the troubled waters of 'values' and 'totalities.' " [2] As Heidegger rightly said in 1935 and again in 1953, National Socialism was "the encounter between global technology and modern man."

I would add that this "encounter" was rather different than Heidegger saw it, or than the contemporary readers of Heidegger might wish to think he saw it. What National Socialism discovered in its encounter with technology was that it could connect technology to mythical consciousness and make this combination the basis of the state. In this way all need for fishing in the troubled waters of values could be eliminated. In this way all persons could be engaged in a total process of state life. The world of the "pure practitioner" and the "disinterested functionary" could hold sway. Cassirer has shown this in *The Myth of the State* (1946) and more specifically in his essay on "The Technique of Our Modern Political Myths" (1945).

Cassirer says of the designers of the National Socialist state: "They knew their way very well and watched every step. From now on myth was no longer allowed to grow up freely and indifferently. The new political myths were by no means wild fruits of an exuberant imagination. They were artificial things made by very skillful and cunning artisans. To put it bluntly we may say that what we see here before our very eyes is a new type of a completely rationalized myth. The twentieth century developed a *technique* of mythical thought which had no equal in previous history. Henceforth myths were invented and manufactured in the same sense and according to the same methods as machine guns or airplanes. And they were used for the same purpose, for internal and external warfare. This was an altogether unprecedented fact, a fact which has changed the whole face of our modern political life." [3]

This state of animals can include empire builders, Nazis, executives, pure researchers, and others who work with the "matter in hand." Hegel says the kind of self involved here is one that "is simply in a reciprocal relation with itself" (Miller, 398). Hegel explains this by an analogy, and he continues: "Just as in the case of indeterminate animal life, which breathes the breath of life, let us say, into the element of water, or air or earth, and within these again into more specific principles, steeping its entire nature in them, and yet keeping that nature under its own control, and preserving itself as a unity, in spite of the limitation imposed by the element, and remaining in the form of this particular organization the same general animal life" (ibid.). The spiritual animal kingdom, the *geistige Tierreich,* means a kind of general spirit or sense of things that holds the animal kingdom together. The animal kingdom does not really mean anything in and of itself. It works toward no particular end, yet each of its forms of life is completely concerned with its own matter in hand—the performance of its own types of activity. But there is no overall goal to the animal kingdom in itself except to perpetuate itself. It is just the activity of its own form of activity. It is "a Nothing working towards Nothing" (Miller, 401).

In this world there are no real goals. There is just the business itself to be attended to. There are only immediate goals. There are no ethical or teleological directions. There can be nothing beyond the self's reciprocal relationship to itself, a nothing working away at nothing. The self here is completely in its own work, its activity. There are no formulated goals toward which the work of all the individual selves point or toward which they are dedicated. What lies beyond their individuality is only the general spirit of things, a kind of medium through which they all relate but which does not function as an end or a goal. Each pursues the practical thing of his choice and believes it to be his own unique form of being. But all choices are really just variations on the thing at hand, just specific courses of action in a general medium of action. They are all just *activities* of one sort or another. Thus there is a humbug of choice. All this individuality and working together is just deception. The individual can never really choose because he cannot choose not to be active with the thing at hand. He must choose one cause or another as his work. There can never be working together because the individual, if he is not to be nothing, must cling to his cause—the "mineness" he can work out in relation to the practical thing. But since all individuals are busy and active, they find themselves thrown together in fields of their activity.

Hegel says: "But the distinction between a content, which is explicit *for* consciousness only *within consciousness itself,* and an intrinsic reality outside it, no longer exists" (Miller, 401). In other words, nature as external to the individual makes no sense. Also it makes no sense for the individual to believe that he has a nature. Human nature makes no sense. What is real is activity itself. Hegel says: "Accordingly, an individual cannot know what he [really] is until he has made himself a reality through action" (ibid.). This is Hegel's statement of the principle of existentialism, that existence precedes essence. In the world of the matter in hand everyone is an existentialist, everyone makes his essence through his sphere of activity. Everyone is anxious, has dread, because activity is nothing working away at nothing. It is not possible to specify the end or goal of this activity, apart from the specific aim of some individual project. We cannot say what human activity as such means. It is nothing. The individual experiences his being as nothing. He is just his activity, just his project at hand—waiting on his tables in the café, or seducing his companion in off-hours. The deception here is continual self-deception because the self cannot say to itself what it is, apart from one of its roles. This is because the human world, like the animal kingdom, is just a general field of activity, with itself as its own end. It is just a field of reciprocal activity.

The existentialist doctrine of the self makes sense in the technological form of society and consciousness. The medium of the technological world is *technique*. All activity is held together by technique, everything is a procedure. In the technological society all individuals are engaged in activity and this activity is part of the general field of activity that is the technological society itself. Herbert Marcuse says: "In the medium of technology, culture, politics, and the economy merge into an omnipresent system which swallows up or repulses all alternatives." [4] Karl Jaspers says: "In our epoch of the mass-order, of technique, of economics, when an attempt is made to render this inevitable institution absolute, there is a danger to the selfhood that the fundamental basis of mind may be destroyed." [5]

In technological society good and bad judgments make no sense. What makes sense is achievement. Hegel says: "In contrast with this unessential *quantitative* [comparing one individual's work with another] difference, 'good' and 'bad' would express an absolute difference; but here this is not in place. Whether something is held to be good or bad, it is in either case an action and an activity in which an individuality exhibits and expresses itself, and for that reason it is all good; and it would, strictly speaking, be impossible to say what 'badness' was supposed to be" (Miller, 403). The individual is just potentiality for action, and action in which there is no failure, anymore than an animal in the animal kingdom can fail at being an animal. It does what it does. Any species engages in the activity suitable to itself as species. Hegel says the individual "can have only the consciousness of the simple transference *of himself* from the night of possibility into the daylight of the present" (Miller, 404). He can *"experience only joy in himself"* (ibid.). The individual has no basis from which to judge himself in terms of good or bad. He is a performer. As he experiences himself in action he cannot but be happy with himself. The technician whistles while he works.

In his classic study, *La Technique ou l'enjeu du siècle* (translated title, *The Technological Society*), Jacques Ellul says: "There is no personal choice, in respect to magnitude, between, say, 3 and 4; 4 is greater than 3; this is a fact which has no personal reference. No one can change it or assert the contrary or personally escape it. Similarly, there is no choice between two technical methods. One of them asserts itself inescapably: its results are calculated, measured, obvious, and indisputable." [6] To the self in reciprocal relationship with itself moral judgments make no more sense than they do in the technological universe. Ellul says: "Technique never observes the distinction between moral and immoral use. It tends, on the contrary, to create a completely independent technical morality. . . . Not even the moral conversion of the technicians could make a difference. At best, they would cease to be good technicians. This attitude [that technique could be used for good or ill purposes] supposes further that technique evolves with some end in view, and that this end is human good. Technique, as I believe I have shown, is totally irrelevant to this notion and pursues no end, professed or unprofessed." [7]

Purpose makes no sense to the self that is joyfully engaged in its own activity in a world that it feels to be at its command. In the technological society the notions of nature or the external world make no sense because the entire object is felt to be at the disposal of technique. Moral judgments or moral ends are irrelevant because the object shows no resistance. There is nothing to oppose the self in its rational activity, that is, in its activity of using reason as a means. In a world in which all is functional, the ethical judgment makes no sense. There is only activity and there is nothing beyond the circle of activity.

The technological society is a world in which there is no ethics and no true individuality but in which there is continually the claim of individuality. There is sustained emphasis on the individual. Each individual has its own cause, has its own role, its own matter in hand. Yet each is really nothing but activity and is unable to take a genuine interest in the activity of other individuals. Everywhere there is talk of the individual but nowhere is there real respect for the individual. Hegel says: "There thus enters a play of individualities with one another in which each and all find themselves both deceiving and deceived" (Miller, 416). Individuals feign interest in each other in an effort to make the practical thing a mine for them individually. Hegel says: "A consciousness that opens up a subject-matter soon learns that others hurry along like flies to freshly poured-out milk, and want to busy themselves with it; and they learn about that individual that he, too, is concerned with the subject-matter, not as an *object,* but as his *own* affair" (Miller, 418). The individuals in this stage sense that they command no substantial reality in themselves, that they are just role-playing and they will play any role they can just to appear successful and real to themselves.

Ellul says of the status of the rights of individuals in technological society: "Modern society is, in fact, conducted on the basis of purely technical considerations. But when men found themselves going counter to the human factor, they reintroduced—and in an absurd way—all manner of moral theories related to the rights of man, the League of Nations, liberty, justice. None of that has any more importance than the ruffled sunshade of McCormick's first reaper. When these moral flourishes overly encumber technical progress, they are discarded—more or less speedily, with more or less ceremony, but with determination nonetheless. This is the state we are in today." [8] In the spiritual animal kingdom any doctrine of individuality or individual rights is a deception. No empire builder, disinterested Nazi, executive, or pure researcher takes ethics seriously or individual rights seriously. What really determines the nature of things is the medium through which everything takes place—technique. Technique is just another name for the matter in hand. It is a specific notion of the matter in hand. Hegel says: "Rather is its nature such that its *being* is the *action* of the *single* individual and of all individuals and whose action is immediately *for others*, or is a 'matter in hand' and is such only as the action of *each* and *everyone*: the essence which is the essence of all beings, viz. *spiritual essence*. Consciousness learns that no one of these moments is *subject*, but rather gets dissolved in the *universal 'matter in hand'*" (Miller, 418).

The matter in hand, like technique, dominates the activity of the individual. No genuine sense of the self is possible. All theories of the self or of rights are just projects of thought, just matters in hand. Thus we can expect as part of the self-deception, the humbug, of this level of consciousness, the production of all sorts of theories of justice, applied ethics, doctrines of individual creativity, plans for world peace, studies of public policy, debates on moral issues. These are all just matters in hand. They are just so much research that keeps the individual engaged, that give the individual his own version of the universal matter in hand, which is just engagement itself.

I wish now to turn to the question of the sense in which this section on the spiritual animal kingdom has a significance for Hegel's project in the *Phenomenology* as a whole. I mentioned earlier that the context in which Hegel is most immediately setting this section is the "animalism" of the world of scholarly research. He has in mind a kind of intellectual pip-squeakism in which "a consciousness that opens up a subject-matter soon learns that others hurry along like flies to freshly poured-out milk." If we relate this to the theme that Hegel has been developing, concerning the philosophical standpoint of mind in stages such as the Master-Servant, Phrenology, etc., we see that he is here adding a footnote to it.

Applied directly to philosophical thought, Hegel is here showing the limits of specialism in philosophy. To be a specialist in philosophy is to be a Hegelian, namely, to become an expert in some particular aspect of Hegel's philosophy or texts and to join with other Hegelians who are also interested in their own expertise. Or it is to become a phenomenologist in the contemporary sense, to join a philosophical movement and become a co-worker in the *cause*. Or, it is to become a hermeneuticist, or an analytic philosopher, or to join any other sort of philosophical school. When philosophy is formed in the manner of schools it can "make discoveries," solve problems, make advances. Philosophy is then not thought of as reality, but as a form of technical work. It pursues various senses of the matter in hand. Philosophy can then join forces with various contemporary social concerns. There can be fashions in philosophical thought and cycles of philosophical problems. The matters in hand of society can become matters in hand for philosophy. Philosophy can be put to work as an instrument for the common good. Philosophy can gain respect because it, like all else, is a specialized activity. It can join with other disciplines and work with them in common on delicate and deep problems. There is no end to the help philosophy can give. It is, however, all humbug.

In Hegel's view philosophy could never be involved with the practical thing, with the cause, the matter in hand. Philosophy is an attempt to think spirit from its own perspective. This requires that we seek the perspective of absolute knowing. All other forms of knowing are deceptions, humbuggery. For philosophy to identify itself with one or all of these is for it to settle itself into a shape of appearance. Philosophical thought must recognize all forms of consciousness as less than the whole, as less than the true. The activity through which philosophical thought liberates itself is phenomenological science of the whole. This is not a matter in hand because it has no specific object as mine. It, in fact, begins by knowing the truth of *das Meinen,* the truth that language can never fully state what is present. It is just this sense of truth that constitutes absolute knowledge. Every stage in the *Phenomenology* is in general terms a matter at hand, because every stage believes it is the essence of consciousness. But when consciousness goes about its work on a given stage it discovers it is really involved in a certain kind of deception. Phenomenology, the doctrine of appearance, would save philosophical thought from itself, being nothing more than the reflections of various of these deceptions. To be a Hegelian would be to take Hegel's thought up as a matter in hand and to make discoveries about it. To attempt to think Hegel's project through would be to try to attain the sense of philosophy as absolute knowing that Hegel teaches. Hegel's *Phenomenology* is instruction in the fact that the true cannot be captured in language or in any particular form of the true. Hegel's thought thus has at its basis a paradox that is intolerable to any mentality concerned with matters in hand.

I wish to turn now to some remarks on the beautiful soul and its connection to the world of the spiritual animal kingdom. The spiritual animal kingdom falls at the end of Hegel's chapter on Reason. It marks the end of reason, the depths to which reason can fall when made the sum and substance of the self's existence. The beautiful soul marks the end of Hegel's chapter on Spirit. The beautiful soul is the low point of spirit's attempt to have man exist as a social animal. The worlds of ethical order *(Sittlichkeit)* and culture *(Bildung)* have progressed within the general form of spirit to a deliberate moral outlook in which spirit is certain of itself *(Moralität)*. In the beautiful soul, the *schöne Seele,* the social animal withdraws into itself: "It lives in dread of besmirching the splendour of its inner being by action and an existence; and, in order to preserve the purity of its heart, it flees from contact with the actual world. . . . The hollow object which it has produced for itself now fills it, therefore, with a sense of emptiness" (Miller, 658).

Hegel has specifically in mind here, as an example of this form of consciousness, the beautiful soul of the Romantic movement. In the background of this section is the portrait of the beautiful soul of the sixth book of Goethe's *Wilhelm Meisters Lehrjahre*. Hegel also has in mind Novalis (1772–1801), the poetic figure of early Romanticism. The beautiful soul was a human type widely known in eighteenth-century Germany, generated by the religious revival of Pietism, that took the form both of living examples of Pietistic "saints" and of well-known Pietistic confessional autobiographies.

The beautiful soul occupies Hegel in his early writings interpreting Christianity as a religion of love in the 1790s. H. S. Harris says: "The community of beautiful souls is marred by any activity that sets one of them or any group of them apart from the rest. All that they can really do together is to eat and drink to maintain life; and all that any of them can do on behalf of the community as a whole is to 'preach the Gospel'. . . . But the zeal for purity and for the Gospel is easily corrupted into fanaticism and persecution: Jesus himself was betrayed by one of the supposedly pure souls." [9] In a recent article discussing the relation of the soul in the *Lehrjahre* and the *Phenomenology*, Benjamin Sax points out that Goethe and Hegel, in their versions of the beautiful, combined Christian notions with Greek: "Reformulating an originally Pietistic self-conception, they combined in this figure specifically Christian notions of 'conscience' *(Gewissen)* and 'heart' *(Herz)* with what they considered a particularly Greek form of acceptance and even love of nature and the world." [10]

Novalis, in *Heinrich von Ofterdingen,* sees the modern age as fragmented. The poet can intuitively grasp the meanings hidden behind the world as we find it in its fragmentation: "Poetry is true Idealism—viewing the world, as viewing a great mind—self-consciousness of the universe." [11] The poet withdraws and can see the nature of the real that cannot be conceptualized. There is no mediation between the infinite that is real and the finite world in which the ordinary self lives. This is why Hegel says of the beautiful soul that "it is the fluctuating attitude to itself of the Unhappy Consciousness; but here this fluctuation takes place explicitly for consciousness within itself, and is conscious of being the concept of Reason, whereas the Unhappy Consciousness is only *implicitly* that concept" (Miller, 658).

Of Novalis, Hegel makes his second most aggressive comment in the *Phenomenology* (equal to his threat to beat in the heads of phrenologists): "Thus the 'beautiful soul', being conscious of this contradiction in its unreconciled immediacy, is unhinged, disordered, and runs to madness, wastes itself in yearning, and pines away in consumption. Thereby it gives up, as a fact, its stubborn insistence on its own isolated self-existence, but only to bring forth the soulless, spiritless unity of abstract being" (Baillie, p. 676; in Miller, 668). As Baillie notes, consumption was the actual fate of Novalis. Why is Hegel so nasty? The standpoint of the beautiful soul, like phrenology, is in a special contest with true speculative philosophy. Phrenology is a threat to philosophy from the side of the object. It purports to reveal the nature of self-consciousness through a science of the spirit as object. The beautiful soul threatens philosophy from the side of the subject. It purports to have a true doctrine of self-consciousness by reducing spirit to pure inwardness. Both of these standpoints contest with philosophy itself.

The beautiful soul is morally and intellectually dangerous because it has a degenerate version of the relation of self-consciousness to the absolute. Its illusion about the absolute is more grave as an obstacle for the self to find the pathway of true speculative thought than that of the earlier Unhappy Consciousness. At this earlier stage, consciousness can become unhappy. The beautiful soul, on the other hand, is happy, self-satisfied, and appears to be the most profoundly poetic, religious, and philosophical of all positions. It appears to be deeply human, to be the authentic self. Instead, it is anti-communal and its drive for purity (or authenticity) is the condition for fanaticism and the destruction of love. Never having understood community, such a beautiful self does not understand how the community of selves offsets death, affirms the reality of community, and survives what the individual self cannot. Let us wish it its abstract, authentic death.

The beautiful soul is the unhappy consciousness that has passed through reason. Reason has shown it that the infinite is just something to cultivate in itself apart from the finitude, the specific activity, of the world. The beautiful soul as such is a personality type. It is a delicate creature that cannot act but can have strong pronouncements in language about what goes on around it. It will judge events, but only in language. It cannot act. The beautiful soul is not difficult to understand, as Hegel sketches it in the several pages he devotes to it. We are familiar in ordinary experience with types of persons that approximate to the stance of the beautiful soul, that is, if we keep polite company and associate from time to time with delicate people. But the implications of Hegel's beautiful soul are wider than this personality portrait.

I suggest that the conception of the beautiful soul tells us something of the being of meditative thought in contemporary technological society. In Hegel's thought the course followed by consciousness goes in a circle that comes back upon itself. Thus we can expect that the end point of reason may have some particular relationship to the end point of spirit. Reason has created the self that is involved in the project, in the matter in hand. It is a world less than human, an animal-like dedication to activity that is meaningless. If we imagine the self—now certain of its self as a fully social self, a social animal that has the experience of *Bildung* and *Sittlichkeit* and even moral duties behind it—facing the world of the matter in hand, we have a concept of the humanist as beautiful soul.

Because of the principle of *Aufhebung* in the science of the experience of consciousness, we know that the world of spirit is built up in opposition to the world of reason. Reason is not left behind but is the element of resistance out of which the social forms of spirit develop. Specifically they develop in contrast to the selfhood of reason—the self as activity engaged in the matter at hand. At the point of the beautiful soul, spirit simply gives in to this resistance by retreating into itself. It now engages in thought, in the contemplating of being, in apprehending its own inner lights, its own authentic existence. It becomes simply very sensitive. Instead of the pip-squeakism of intellectual discoveries, it becomes profound and seeks the light. It wishes to be authentic. It will have nothing to do with the world of the empire builders, the Nazis, the American executives, the scientists. It will retreat to its own special place and issue its statements.

From this perspective philosophy becomes meditative thinking, in opposition to the mundane thought of the matter in hand. There is an atmosphere of conscience and duty and, in fact, of culture; but they have been left behind. They are parts of existence against which it must struggle to keep its sights on the inner access to infinitude. There is nothing to be done but to wait and watch and be ready for some moment of special understanding. There is no possibility for love or *eros.* No Socratic element is possible for it. Language can be used in only · a revelatory fashion. Statements can be made but dialogue is impossible. The basis of philosophy here is silence and solitude. Poetic dwelling and indwelling is the basic form of thought.

The bacchanalian revel of the forms of the *Phenomenology* is closed to the philosophy of the beautiful soul because such a soul has not and cannot have a sense of humor. Irony, through which appearances are laid open, is not a meaningful thought for it (although Novalis would allow for this). The beautiful soul takes itself seriously, so seriously it has left the world for itself. Each stage of the *Phenomenology,* when it becomes the basis of a philosophical position, involves forgetting the rest of the whole. This self has remembered the unhappy consciousness but has forgotten the inverted world, the principle of topsy-turvy. Having gotten full into itself it cannot determine how to get back out of itself. Since it is self-consciousness certain of itself as spirit it does not require the mediation of the third party of the original unhappy consciousness and it can simply meditate on its finitude and infinitude.

The beautiful soul can live in the world of the spiritual animal kingdom and the kingdom can easily go on with its activity with the beautiful soul around. Both are sufficiently defective forms of selfhood to be ineffective against each other. In fact, the beautiful soul is in principle understandable to the self of the matter in hand. The beautiful soul is simply activity, but it is purely spiritual activity. Its object is not external in the sense of a cause, a particular business to be done. The beautiful soul's business is itself in relation to its personal sense of the infinite or unchangeable being. The self of the matter in hand can understand this in principle because it is just a kind of activity. It cannot imagine what this spiritual inner activity would be like or why anyone would want to make it its business. But it knows instinctively that this beautiful activity is harmless to the real world in which it is active. Indeed, if the animal kingdom were asked what it thinks philosophy to be (not what the animal kingdom would like philosophy to be, something it could make use of, etc.), it would reply with a description of the beautiful soul.

Nine

Religion versus Absolute Knowing

The last chapter of the *Phenomenology,* "Das absolute Wissen," is usually passed through quickly by commentators and students of Hegel. It is one of the shortest chapters in the *Phenomenology,* somewhat longer than either the first or the second chapter. I agree with Merold Westphal's acute comment: "Complaints about its tantalizing brevity (with the usual explanations about the conditions under which the manuscript was completed) may reflect more on the critic's attention to the text than on Hegel's ability to say what he meant." [1] But it appears very brief to the reader who has just gone through the massive chapters of Reason and Spirit and Hegel's substantial treatment of religion. Even though Hegel was supposedly writing this last chapter as Napoleon's army approached Jena, as the much-awaited, final and direct explanation of absolute knowing, it seems rather slight and abstract—an anticlimax.

By this point most of Hegel's philosophical readers, his prisoners of the passage, are busy preparing to leave Hegel's many-cabined Ship of Fools, with its halls of mirrors and dead-end corridors. Sanity awaits them. They are looking forward to the promised smooth journey of categories in the realm of pure thought of the *Logic.* Its timelessness beckons them on. The possibility of being able to think the concept in terms of itself makes them grow keen with anticipation and their hearts beat faster. The word is passed among them that "what absolute knowing is, is in the *Logic.*" Hegel has tried our patience long enough and we are ready to think without all the phantasmagoria of the *Phenomenology.* The *Logic* waits for us like a familiar adventure.

Hegel's conception of absolute knowing in the *Phenomenology* is usually dealt with in terms of a single idea, which Hegel states in the second sentence of the chapter: "The *content* of this picture-thinking *[des Vorstellens]* is absolute Spirit; and all that now remains to be done is to supersede *[das Aufheben]* this mere form . . ." (Miller, 788). In the stage of revealed religion, consciousness has reached the level of absolute spirit in *content* but this stage is defective in *form*. In revealed religion the content of absolute spirit is presented in pictorial form *(Vorstellung)* and not in purely conceptual form, not in the form of the *Begriff* itself. The truth is presented in scriptural language, using images of the Christ, the Father, etc. These images point beyond themselves to the truth that they do not literally express. As absolute knowing consciousness must go to that level of absolute spirit to which the thought of revealed religion can only point, and it must think these meanings in terms of themselves. This account of the chapter on absolute knowing is easily grasped; it has the ring of an oft-told tale. From this tale comes the proverbial statement about Hegel's philosophy that imagistic thinking, *Vorstellung,* is abhorrent to Hegel because his philosophy, unlike other philosophies, is the thought of the concrete concept.

What is the nature of the *Aufhebung* between religion and absolute knowing? Is it a matter of the simple adjustment of content and form, a kind of final refinement of a process nearly brought to completion in the stage of revealed religion? Or is there something traumatic in the shift from religion to absolute knowing? *Aufhebung,* as Hegel uses it, means both to preserve and to cancel or annul. The standard tale of the relationship between religious consciousness and absolute knowing focuses on the preservation side of this term. Absolute knowing preserves the content of religion, that to which its scriptural speech refers, and adds to it the proper conceptual form. It replaces the scriptural image with the concretely developed logical category. Now we have the notion of absolute knowing as something in itself—the idea of the thought of thought. Cancelling here has meant only the request that the scriptural image step aside and make room for the category.

I think something much stronger has gone on and must go on if absolute knowing is to be understood as something more than conceptualized religion (a view with which not all readers of Hegel would be unhappy). I suggest that there must be a real difference between absolute knowing and religion and in fact there must be a real and present difference between absolute knowing and all other stages of the *Phenomenology.* If this is not so, then absolute knowing is just another stage in the science of the experience of consciousness, and not the science itself. To put this simply, every stage of consciousness described in the *Phenomenology* is an illusion, a trap, a *Verwicklung,* an entanglement, a confusion, an embarrassment, of consciousness. This occurs because at each stage consciousness believes that it has found reality. It believes that it has mastered appearance and discovered the key to the real. But this discovery, as it attempts to work out its details and its supposed power, turns into an embarrassment, a confusion. It has been deluded. But it learns very little from this experience. Optimistically it grasps another master key to reality and asserts it, dedicates itself to this new understanding of the object and itself. Consciousness illustrates Hegel's statement about our relationship to history: that history teaches only one thing, that we learn nothing from history. In moving from one stage to the next in this fashion, consciousness never learns anything so general as this truth. It forgets the general truth of its path, it fails to see that it is on a highway of despair and, simply taking up what it can preserve of the exhausted stage it has just been through, it sets to work to build the next disappointment for itself, all the while believing it now must truly have the problem solved.

Traditionally we are told that as we move up the stages of the *Phenomenology* subject and object move closer and closer toward a unity with each other. Consciousness more and more recognizes its object as itself. The *Phenomenology* is thought to be like a pyramid in which the sides that are wide apart at its base increase to their union at its point. Subject and object are like lines that are wide apart at the beginning and which approach each other to a point in absolute knowing. Absolute knowing is the highest degree of integration (a unity-in-difference) between subject and object. But how does absolute knowing differ from the other stages before it? Does it differ just in the degree of unity it exhibits? Then there is no real difference between absolute knowing and the stages that are not absolute. On this view absolute knowing is just more of the same of what is striven for on each stage. On such a view we are unable to say what the real difference is between absolute knowing and any other stage.

What is it that each stage believes it has found the key to? It believes it has discovered the way to unite the two moments that it first experienced as sense-certainty, and which Hegel describes in his introduction as the moments of his method. These are what I have called the two senses of *Ansich*—the in-itself and the in-itself as something for consciousness. Each stage of consciousness announces that it has found the key to merging these two moments. Each believes that there is something that these two moments have *in common,* that there is some type of relationship that they share. Thus consciousness, for example, announces variously that these two senses of *Ansich* are just both aspects of the thing, or of a struggle between selves, or of observational reason, or of social and moral life, or of religious awareness. In each of these forms consciousness claims to have discovered the principle of transforming this double sense of *Ansich* into a *unity* that is in and for itself. But what it receives for its efforts is only a false sense of unity. What it seeks is a notion of unity that is literally an *An-für-sichsein*. It seeks an identity-in-difference in which the moments of the in itself will be unified by some type of relation, some principle of relationship that as a for itself holds this structure of being together as one.

What each such stage that is not absolute knowing has missed is the true meaning of the conjunction—and *(und)*—in the in and for itself, *an und für sich*. Each stage of consciousness has fled from the simple conjunction of these two moments and attempted to replace the conjunction with some sense of their identity, with something that makes them aspects of the same thing. Each stage of consciousness fails because it *forgets* about the *and*. It fails to recall the presence of *andness* in the structure in and for itself. It only recalls the two extremes and searches for their union. Hegel says: "the power of Spirit lies rather in remaining the selfsame Spirit in its externalization and, as that which is both *in itself* and *for itself*, in making its *being-for-self* no less merely a moment than its in-itself; nor is Spirit a *tertium quid* that casts the differences back into the abyss of the Absolute and declares that therein they are all the same; on the contrary, knowing is this seeming inactivity which merely contemplates how what is differentiated spontaneously moves in its own self and returns into its unity *[Einheit]* " (Miller, 804).

Spirit is not a *tertium quid* (Hegel's term is *ein Drittes*). It is not a third something, a term that is to be discovered as something in addition to the two original terms of in itself and for itself. Spirit makes its *being-for-self*, its *Fürsichsein*, by simply being this moment as well as being an *Ansichsein*. Spirit is not a third term in which the in itself and the for itself are united. Spirit is just the movement between these two poles of itself. If we ask what is spirit, the answer is the account of this movement. Spirit is nothing in addition. It is not a third something in which the other two terms exist. Hegel calls spirit a unity *(Einheit)* at the same time that he denies that spirit is a third. Thus Hegel's notion of unity is completely process-like. The in itself and the in itself for consciousness that is a for itself, these two moments, are held together by nothing; but they always, that is, by necessity, accompany each other. One is the meaning of the other. What is absolute is not something that as unity is their goal, an end point of oneness toward which they develop. What is absolute is what is between them—the absolute gap that separates them as absolute moments. Spirit is not a third term that offers them an identity-in-difference. Hegel's notion of unity here is just the notion of a twoness that can never be compressed into a oneness.

Absolute knowing is the recognition, the recollection of the and, the *und,* in the combination *An-* und *Fürsichsein.* The absolute is not a goal of this double-termed expression. The absolute is what is between the two terms, the absolute distance that cannot be reduced between them. The absolute spirit is inside the in and for itself, not outside. Every stage in the *Phenomenology* has been an attempt, an attempt that has ended in failure and embarrassment, to deny this fact of the *internal absolute,* the genuine separation of the two fundamental moments of consciousness. As the *Phenomenology* progresses, each stage becomes more elaborate in its spinning of illusions; wider and wider contexts are produced by consciousness in its attempt to snare both' these moments in its nets. The grandest of all these snares is religion. Religion is the last grand illusion. Its attempt at a substantive unity between the two moments is nearly successful but it fails to balance *Bild* with *Begriff.* Its unseen or *begriffliche* element is still *bildhaft.* We cannot form the Christ as a thought. The truth of religion is always something to be *vorgestellt* and not *begriffen.* Revealed religion tried to unify the two moments of consciousness by means of a revelation, a kind of immediate presentation of their mutual interdependence. In this presentation *(Vorstellung)* the *and* seems almost to disappear, only to reappear and to continue to do so. The content of this religious consciousness is correct, the sense of mutuality and correspondence *(Entsprechung)* is correct. But it is defective in form because the genuine reality of the *and* is not acknowledged.

Spirit is process-like in that it is just the movement between the two moments of in itself and for itself. As religion it is still substance and not subject. Hegel says: "But this substance which is Spirit is the process in which Spirit *becomes* what it is *in itself;* and it is only as this process of reflecting itself into itself that it is in itself truly *Spirit.* It is in itself the movement which is cognition—the transforming of that *in-itself* into that which is *for itself,* of substance into subject, of the object of *consciousness* into an object of *self-consciousness,* i.e. into an object that is just as much superseded, or into the *concept.* The movement is the circle that returns into itself, the circle that presupposes its beginning and reaches it only at the end" (Miller, 802). In the sentence that introduces these, Hegel says: "For experience is just this, that the content—which is Spirit—is *in itself* substance, and therefore an *object* of *consciousness"* (ibid.). Still on the level of religion spirit is substance *(Substanz)* and not subject *(Subject).* The unity of the two moments is still something to be presented *(vorgestellt).* The in itself and the for itself are still not a circle for consciousness. The *and* has still not been accepted. Consciousness is still having experience *(Erfahrung),* namely, attempting to have the two moments as a unified *object.* It is still attempting to have the difference of the two moments of the Father and the Son in the identity of a third, the Ghost.

Hegel says: "Spirit necessarily appears in Time, and it appears in Time just so long as it has not *grasped* its pure concept, i.e. has not annulled time" (Miller, 801). Spirit appears in time as substance, as the attempt to annul time, to fix a unity between the two moments, but it is unsuccessful. Thus it moves on in time to the next stage. It only annuls time when it accepts the conjunction, the *and,* as fundamental. Now it no longer lives from stage to stage but recollects. Recollection *(Erinnerung)* is a denial of time. When we rethink the course of spirit, we cancel its time. We are the masters of its time. Philosophical knowing is always a denial of time on behalf of the whole. Where there is partiality there is time because there is always a next—the part that is not in the first partial moment. When we recollect we are masters of the whole and we bring each part of the whole into contact with the whole. Philosophical or absolute knowing allows us to be at the point of the whole which is beyond time. Inside the whole is the bad infinity; at the level of the whole is the true *(wahre)* infinity. Recollection is the activity of the true infinite because it is always an activity of bringing forth parts from the whole. The whole of memory itself is always its beginning point. And the language of memory is the image.

Another way to put this is that absolute knowing is wisdom. Kojève says: "Now in Chapter VIII, Hegel is no longer talking about the Philosopher [the *lover* of wisdom], but about the Wise Man *[le Sage]*, about Wisdom." [2] He continues: "All philosophers are in agreement about the *definition* of the Wise Man. Moreover, it is very simple and can be stated in a single sentence: that man is Wise who is capable of answering in a *comprehensible* or satisfactory manner *all* questions that can be asked him concerning his acts, and capable of answering in such fashion that the *entirety* of his answers forms a *coherent* discourse. Or else, what amounts to the same thing: that man is Wise who is *fully* and *perfectly self-conscious.*" [3] What is coherent discourse? What is perfect self-consciousness? Hegel has re-defined both of these. Both are based on his conception of *Erinnerung*. The Wise Man answers all questions not by inventing or projecting new ideas, but by recollecting, by not forgetting, the forms of experience. His *scientia* is his *conscientia*. His "science" is the production in his "conscience" of a discourse that contains all phenomena that can be brought to bear on any question. The Wise Man weds Mnemosyne, the mother of the Muses, who copulates with Zeus. The Philosopher has always aspired to be God.

Cognition is less than absolute knowing because it always has an object. Its object is to unify the in itself, that is before it as the known, with the in itself for it, that is the knower. Absolute knowing, like the ancient notion of wisdom, just accepts what is there. It accepts the absolute distance between the in itself and the for itself. It accepts the circle that is formed through the *and.* This acceptance leaves the world as it is and in this way appearance is conquered. Hegel says: "Whereas in the phenomenology of Spirit each moment is the difference of knowledge and Truth, and is the movement in which that difference is cancelled, Science on the other hand does not contain this difference and the cancelling of it" (Miller, 805). Hegel's science is wisdom. One stage as recollected (this science is a science of recollection) does not cancel the other as it does in the actual experience of consciousness when it is living its illusions.

In the first half of the chapter on absolute knowing, Hegel recollects from this standpoint the various stages of the *Phenomenology*. He even, as Findlay has pointed out, sketches in one long paragraph (Miller, 803) the whole previous history of modern philosophy (see also Findlay's commentary on this paragraph, Miller, p. 591).[4] Hegel's chapter on absolute knowing is a compressed piece of recollection. This chapter is not understandable unless this fact is seen, and it cannot be seen unless we have already taken up Hegel's description of his science as recollective, as stated in the final paragraph of the *Phenomenology*. In his recollection of the stages of the work, Hegel brings attention back to the beautiful soul, and in fact brings us back to this stage slightly out of its earlier order. Hegel says: "The 'beautiful soul' is its own knowledge of itself in its pure, transparent unity— the self-consciousness that knows this pure knowledge of *pure inwardness* as Spirit. It is not only the intuition of the Divine but the Divine's intuition of itself" (Miller, 795).

Why does Hegel emphasize the beautiful soul here? His recollection of other stages is much more generally stated. I think this is because the beautiful soul is very close to the philosophical standpoint of absolute knowing. When the self steps from its final role as substance in the form of revealed religion into the self as subject, it risks confusion and forgetfulness. It can revert here to the corresponding end stage of *Geist*—the life of the beautiful soul. Hegel says: "Thus, what in religion was *content* or a form for presenting an *other,* is here the *self's* own *act* [ist heir eignes *Tun* des *Selbsts*]; the concept requires the *content* to be the *Self's* own act [eignes *Tun* des *Selbsts* ist] " (Miller, 797).

The risk here is great that the self, in making itself into its own act, will forget the *experience* of itself as the beautiful soul and fall back to its position, perhaps tying itself up in a series of oppositions to all the end points of the major stages of the *Phenomenology,* juxtaposing itself to the spiritual animal kingdom, to the unhappy consciousness (with which it shares a certain interest in the infinite), to the *verkehrte Welt* and the deception of the thing (principles that it could apply to its judgments on the corruption of the spiritual animal kingdom), all the way back to the *Meinen* of sense-certainty. For consciousness to retreat into a position of philosophical mineness now would bring down the structure of the *Phenomenology* like a house of cards. Philosophy would settle for the appearance of wisdom by retreating into itself, into its act of thought. It would just allow thought to "come over it." It would seek its own authenticity apart from the experience of consciousness and would in fact cut itself off from experience. Thought would enter only the house of its own act.

What is the self's own act, *eignes* Tun *des* Selbsts? What is the philosophical act that is absolute knowledge? As the beautiful soul philosophy would forget the first moment of the two senses of in itself. It would attempt to forget the *Ansich* itself and just live as *Fürsich,* as an in and for itself that is just for it. It would attempt to achieve the absolute standpoint of spirit at the cost of one moment. What saves philosophy from this is what Hegel in the first stage of the *Phenomenology,* sense-certainty, called the "divine nature" of language, its *göttliche Natur.* As Hegel says, the beautiful soul is not only the "intuition of the Divine but the Divine's intuition of itself." The beautiful soul believes in poetry and would reduce absolute knowing to the poetic act of the intuition of the divine, to a communion with being in which being is also in communion with itself.

But absolute knowledge requires language and it requires language in all of its dimensions, in its discursive as well as its poetic powers. Absolute knowledge accepts language; it accepts the truth of language learned at the level of *das Meinen*—that the real cannot be said.

The science of the experience of consciousness is a linguistic science and it is a recollective science. It is an act of recollection carried on in language. But this act is a tragic act because language, even poetic language, never speaks the whole. Recollection and the language of recollection keeps us from the philosophical science that is merely an exhaltation of the absolute as a divine to be intuited. It forces us to form the whole as language, to recollect experience. If we give attention to Hegel's very last use of the term recollection *(Erinnerung)* in the last paragraph of the *Phenomenology,* this tragic sense of language and the act of absolute knowing can be seen.

Most commentators see Hegel's final remarks in his presentation of absolute knowing as projections of the further parts of his system, and, indeed, some such correlation can be made. Hegel's remarks about nature and subject in the penultimate paragraph (Miller, 807) have a sense of his distinction between the later philosophy of nature and the philosophy of spirit of the *Encyclopaedia.* They can just as well be read as reflections back into the *Phenomenology* in its course between reason and spirit. From the perspective of absolute knowing these sections have such a significance. I think that Hegel's comments in these final passages are working on two levels at once: they both indicate, in final terms, how to look back at the significance of what has happened in the *Phenomenology,* and they suggest the directions our thought will take if we attempt, not just to reread the *Phenomenology,* but to rethink it, to recollect it and in some way restate it from a new perspective. Hegel's statements here point in two directions at once; they say what the *Phenomenology* is and they hint at what can come out of it—the rest of Hegel's system (and they are hints that should be carefully followed up in reading the rest of Hegel's works).

In the last paragraph of the *Phenomenology,* Hegel says: "The *goal,* absolute knowing, or spirit knowing itself as spirit has for its path the recollection of spirits as they are to themselves and accomplish the organization of their realm. Their preservation on the side of their free existence, appearing in the form of contingency, is history, but on the side of their conceptually grasped organization is the *science* of *the coming into appearance of knowing;* both together, conceptually grasped history, form the recollection and the Calvary of absolute spirit, the reality, truth, and certainty of its throne, without which it would be lifeless solitude; only—from the chalice of this realm of spirits/foams out to Him His infinity" (my trans.). The side of contingency or history is composed of the actual pieces of experience formed in the *Phenomenology.* The side of the science of apparent knowing is the *Phenomenology* proper. Both together are time from the standpoint of the *Begriff,* i.e., conceptualized history. This time is the Calvary of absolute spirit. Absolute spirit annuls time with language, with recollection. But this annulling is tragic. Absolute spirit hangs on its cross because the annulment of time cannot be perfectly accomplished. Spirit does not create its own perfect likeness. Its friendship with its own forms is not complete. They foam out to it and it must recollect them. Experience cannot be perfectly recollected, yet this recollection saves philosophy from the lifeless solitude of the beautiful soul, taken as a description of philosophical life.

The *Phenomenology* ends with an image—Calvary, the throne, the cup foaming forth. This is a final irony. Hegel has said that religion is not absolute knowing because it delivers the content of absolute spirit in the form of picture-thinking *(Vorstellung)*. Now Hegel uses this very form to conclude absolute knowing and the *Phenomenology* itself. How is this final act to be understood? Calvary is an image of an end that is also a beginning. It is an image of suffering and triumph through suffering. It is a master image of opposites—finitude and infinitude and the circle of beginning and end.

By concluding the *Phenomenology* in this way Hegel reminds us that the image is still with us. The *Begriff* still has a connection with the *Bild.* At the level of absolute knowing we can recognize the *Bild,* the image, for what it is, in the same way that we can recognize the absolute difference between the in itself and the in itself for consciousness. The image is the concept as we find it in itself. When we grasp the meaning of the image we take it up as the concept. The problem of the *Phenomenology* has been to make the concept, the *Begriff,* appear to us. We approach the chapter on absolute knowing thinking that it will be unique, because here will be the language of the *Begriff.* But what we learn is a new point of view, an absolute point of view. We learn to distinguish between two senses of thought—that which presents meaning through another medium and that which presents meaning through its own medium. For the philosopher the image, the *Vorstellung* or the *Bild,* must always have a meaning other than itself. It must always be a step toward the *Begriff.* If the image is not this, philosophy does not begin and there is only poetry. The beautiful soul achieves its false philosophical stance because it forgets this truth about the status of the image for philosophy. It then is left with poetry. In so doing it forgets philosophy and pretends its poetry is philosophical, is the true philosophical act.

In the *Phenomenology* the concept always appears in conjunction with the image. As with the in and for itself, we are always presented with the image, the metaphor, and the conceptual account of Hegel's meaning. Even in the last sentence Hegel reminds us of this by his use of the religious imagery that he has just given up. The concept is always being extracted from the image by the developing consciousness in the *Phenomenology.* This consciousness is in a struggle with the image. The image always is required to begin the dialectical development of a meaning. It is the language of the *archai* and the concept is the language of what follows—what shows forth on the basis of the showing forth of the *archai.*

In absolute knowledge we have learned to tell the difference between the two moments of the in itself and the difference between the image and the concept. But we have learned this through recollection *(Erinnerung).* This act of thought that inwardizes allows us only to approach the concept through the image. We recollect in images and bring forth from them their meaning. But our apprehension of the concept is always as an outer to the image. In the recollective act we are in the image. The speculative proposition then draws us out from the image to the dialectical articulation of its meaning. But the conceptual process of the speculative cannot sustain itself and it is taken back to the recollective for its refreshment, for a new sense of beginning. The image always brings meaning; the concept is an attempt to sustain it. But this is a circle. There is always a correspondence between the in itself and the for itself, between the image and the concept. Each takes us back to the other.

The philosophical act of the self as absolute knowing forces it into time. It has no illusions about the opposition of the in itself and the for itself. It accepts their simple conjunction the way no other stage that it recollects can. Yet the true infinity that results from this circle is nonetheless an endlessness. The spirits foam forth carried by language, but language can never say what it means. The whole is a particular individual that must be spoken in language and it can no more be expressed than can the mind of sense-certainty express in the *this* the actual particularity that it senses.

In considering his image of the "True as the Bacchanalian revel" in the preface to the *Phenomenology,* Hegel says: "In the *whole* of the movement, seen as a state of repose, what distinguishes itself therein, and gives itself particular existence, is preserved as something that *recollects* itself [*sich erinnert*], whose existence is self-knowledge, and whose self-knowledge is just as immediately existence" (Miller, 47). Reflection is the tool of modern philosophy which always leaves the self or subject external to the object. Reflection is always only an examination of the examination of the object. It never overcomes the "vacuous actuality" of the object.[5] Hegel's transformation of substance into subject overcomes this vacuous actuality of the object by making the object a moment of the subject's recollection. The object is always a moment of the self's inward movement; it is a moment of its own past. The vacuous actuality that characterizes the nature of the object of reflection is not overcome by giving the object an "inside." It is overcome by making the object itself part of the inside, the actuality of the knowing self. Critical reflection is overcome through the recollective, memorial nature of the speculative act that produces the inward being of the real.

The *Phenomenology* is a comedy for consciousness as it achieves absolute knowing. But its joy turns to a tragic face as it learns that only here does the "highway of despair" begin. The *we* who have all along been called "observers," and who felt a certain sense of our own reality while watching the tribulations of consciousness, now realize Hegel's final irony. The *we,* who were beyond the illusion of any given stage of the *Phenomenology,* now know that they were mistaken about absolute knowing. They had grasped it in only a half-light. Now that they are in its sun, they are no longer observers, but pilgrims on the path of the seen and the unseen. They now must attempt to draw forth the *Begriff* from the *Bild.* They thought it was being done for them. They were, after all, invited to observe, to be the audience. No wonder everyone is hurrying on to the *Logic.* It may be there where we are told the secret of separating the concept from the word. But if we have not learned it here, why can we expect to learn it elsewhere?

Ten

Epilogue

I

My purpose in this work has been to interpret the *Phenomenology* and not to interpret Hegel's whole system. But my views, especially my view of the status of *und* in the formulation of *An- und Fürsichsein* in the stage of *absolutes Wissen,* raise questions about how the major transitions of Hegel's system can be seen. It is beyond my intention to offer an interpretation of how the whole system of Hegel hangs together. But any serious reader of Hegel must have a viewpoint as to how the system works. In the "Preface to the First Edition" of the *Science of Logic* Hegel is quite clear that he regards the *Phenomenology* as the first part of a system of philosophy, the second part containing the logic and the two "realen Wissenschaften der Philosophie"—the philosophy of nature and the philosophy of spirit.[1] How do the major transitions look, given the viewpoint I have taken on the *Phenomenology?*

The great problem in the interconnection of Hegel's works is the transition between the end of the *Logic* and the philosophy of nature. By *Logic* I mean the "larger logic" of the *Science of Logic* and the so-called "lesser logic" of the *Encyclopedia.* There are differences between these two books, but both involve the same question of the position of logic in the system. It has seemed to some readers and critics of Hegel that at this point thought itself, or the absolute idea, becomes nature. Hegel is clear that this is not the case. The movement from idea to nature is not *"a process of becoming" (ein Gewordensein)* nor is it a *"transition" (Übergang)* such as exists within the *Logic,* e. g., as when "the *subjective end becomes life" (der subjektive Zweck zum Leben wird).* The passage here is to be understood through an absolute liberation *(absolute Befreiung),* a freedom *(Freiheit)* that the *Begriff* at this point commands. The "idea *freely releases itself" (die Idee sich selbst frei entlässt).*[2]

115

The key to the passage from Idea to nature lies in the passage from the *Phenomenology* to the *Logic,* a movement that is usually taken for granted. In the view I have espoused, the point consciousness reaches at the stage of absolute knowing can be likened to a state of mind which has no illusions about the possibility of a unity between being in-itself and for-itself. Every preceding stage of consciousness in the *Phenomenology* has attempted to live the illusion that it had found the key to bringing these two moments completely into a unity and eliminating the sense of opposition that is represented by the "and" that exists between them. Absolute knowing is the attainment of the wisdom of which no other stage is capable—namely, that the "and" is real. Absolute knowing differs absolutely from all the other forms of knowing that precede it.

Absolute knowing is the realization that the passage from what is *ansich* to what is *ansich* for us *(für uns)* (or the parallel passage from the standpoint of being from what is *ansich* to what is *fürsich*) is not a process of becoming *(ein Gewordensein)* nor is it a transition *(Übergang)*. The root of the absolute liberation of consciousness, its ground of its freedom, is in the absolute "space" between these two moments. The "and" that exists between them represents not the merger in a unity between these two moments but only that being exists in a state of mutual attachment to itself and, in like fashion, the mind as subject exists in mutual attachment to its object.

Once the illusion of unifying the two moments is overcome in absolute knowing in the *Phenomenology,* way for the *Logic* is made. Wise in the wisdom that from the standpoint of the experience of the object consciousness cannot grasp the unity of the two moments, it can deliberately and willfully attempt to approach the "and" in thought. It can attempt to formulate the "and" as a unity in categoreal terms. What drives the dialectic forward in the *Logic* from Being and Nothing to the absolute Idea is the attempt to think *An- und Fürsichsein* as the single unity: *An-Fürsichsein.* At each stage of the *Logic* thought tests out the possibility of this thought and finds further modification needed. The *Logic* is a discourse on the possible meanings of "and."

The inability of the thought of the *Logic* fully to master this "and" by formulating it as a category is due to the original element of freedom— the irreducibility of what is *ansich* to what is *fürsich* or the reverse. This makes Hegel's "system of science" a circle and in fact, as Hegel says, a circle that is a circle of circles *(ein Kreis von Kreisen):* so that each member returns to its own beginning and is the beginning of the next member. Hegel says at the end of the *Logic* that each one of his sciences in his system of science is joined to the others like links in a chain *(Kette):* "each of which has an *antecedent* and a *successor*—or, expressed more accurately, *has* only the *antecedent* and *indicates* its *successor* in its con- clusion." [3]

This is not that sense of a circle in which once the series of links are linked to themselves the circle becomes a hoop—a smooth, self-enclosed structure. The sense of "links" remains. The moments are *linked* to each other just as what is "in" and what is "for" itself are linked by the "and." Links touch where one ends and the other begins but the ending of one and the beginning of the other are not continuous. There is a "gap," an element that is there and not there. It is part of what makes the chain a chain but it can never be a "moment" in the chain or one of its links. The beginning and end of any two links bound this gap. But it is always absolutely present.

The *circle of circles* is not just true as a description of the second part of the system of science, of the circles of logic, nature, and spirit, it is also true of phenomenology or "science of the experience of consciousness." In the preface to the *Phenomenology* Hegel explains that living substance has being as subject not because of "an *original* unity as such, or an *immediate* unity as such" ("eine *ursprüngliche* Einheit als solche, oder *unmittelbare* als solche") but because it attempts to overcome the "doubling" *(Verdoppelung)* within itself by the circular process. Hegel says: "It is the process of its own becoming, the circle that presupposes its end as its goal, having its end also as its beginning; and only by being worked out to its end, is it actual" (Miller, 18; Hoffmeister, p. 20).

The reason Hegel can so easily and simply say that nature follows from the Idea at the end of the *Logic* by the Idea "freely releasing itself" is because that is exactly how substance as subject effects its passage into Being, the first category of the *Logic.* Absolute knowing freely releases itself into the world of metaphysical thought, not because it has attained a unity between the two moments within the being of the subject, but because it has overcome all illusion that there is such a *phenomenon.* It takes up the quest for unity in different terms; it attempts to *think* the "and" of its two moments as a unity. In the last paragraph of the *Logic* Hegel says, "The Idea, namely, in positing itself as absolute *unity [Einheit]* of the pure concept *[Begriff]* and its reality and thus contracting itself into the immediacy of *being,* is the *totality* in this form—*nature.*" [4] With the Idea we are back to the question of unity which has not been answered, and the circle must begin again as nature.

In the circles of the links of the circular chain of Hegel's system of science the "and" is always present as the connection between the links. "The True is the whole" (Miller, 20). But the unity of the whole remains always problematic. Carl Vaught, in *The Quest for Wholeness,* has expressed this sense of openness and otherness that exists within the Hegelian system when it is approached through the *Phenomenology* and in terms of the metaphor.

> To say that the world as a whole is a dynamic process of development
> is to use a cosmic metaphor, the richness of which stands behind any of
> Hegel's more particular attempts to articulate the significance of the Whole
> in systematic terms. It is in this sense that a metaphorical dimension lies
> at the foundation of Hegel's system and provides the ground of his quest
> for absolute comprehension.
>
> Since metaphors are open-ended and since the concept of the Whole is
> a metaphorical extension from finite contexts of cognition, mystery and
> indeterminacy are present in the concept of the Whole as Hegel introduces
> it. . . . In fact, the stages generated by Hegel's philosophical quest for
> completeness can be regarded as a sequence of metaphors which are held
> together by analogical connections.[5]

This could not be more correct. The metaphor is there throughout Hegel's
system, both in its very conception and in the way it is expressed in the
text. In the view I have advanced the "and" is what makes possible the
analogical element.

The passage between the *Phenomenology* and the *Logic* is the passage
between what is *ansich* and what is *fürsich* writ large. These works stand
to each other as *An-und Fürsichsein*. To say now, as most commentators
would, that *An-und Fürsichsein* represents the idea of a "self-differentiated
unity" is to explain nothing of the sense of difference that is required
between the two moments that are held together with the "and" *(und)*.
It is to minimize the reality of the "and" in the experience of consciousness
and, most of all, it is to fail to account for how the stage of absolute
knowing is genuinely different from all the stages preceding it.

II

In the end, irony, as well as metaphor and recollection, is the key to
Hegel's system, both in his style of writing and in the presence of the
"and" with which his system struggles and which leads it on from link to
link. In this irony Hegel is in a great tradition, as it is the device of
philosophers of self-knowledge from the founding of such philosophy with
Socrates.

In his little manuscript entitled *Wer denkt abstrakt?* ("Who Thinks
Abstractly?"),[6] written in April 1807 or shortly thereafter, just about the
time of the appearance of the first printed copies of the *Phenomenology,*
Hegel gives a clue to how to understand his thought. He says: "Let those
who can save themselves!" He says he has no ambition to instruct the
world against its will. He intends to make his purpose clear from the
beginning. Hegel has his "metaphysical overcoat" *(metaphysischer Überrock)*
open from the start. The flashing star of wisdom—the absolute—is there.

A *docta ignorantia* is required in order to work the buttons. A sense of ignorance and the irony of the human condition are required or we may simply mistake conventional understanding for wisdom. We may stop on one of the stages of the *Phenomenology* and think it is the end.

Bertolt Brecht, during his years of exile from Germany, wrote the following in his curious little work, *Flüchtlingsgespräche* (Refugee dialogues), on how to understand Hegel. Ziffel speaks for Brecht.

Ziffel

Concerning humor I always think of the philosopher Hegel, something I picked up in the library; thus I am able to respond to you philosophically.

Kalle

Tell me about it. I am not educated enough that I read him myself.

Ziffel

He had the stuff of one of the greatest humorists among philosophers; Socrates is the only other one who had a similar method. But Hegel had seemingly bad luck and was employed in Prussia and sold himself to the state. However, eye twinkling was innate to him, so far as I can see, like a birth defect and he had it until death; without being conscious of it he continuously blinked his eyes like someone with St. Vitus's dance. He had such humor that he could never think of something like order, for example, without disorder. It was clear to him that right next to the greatest order dwells the greatest disorder; he went so far that he even said—in one and the same place! By the state he understood something that originates just where the sharpest opposites between classes appear, so that, so to say, the harmony of the state lives through the disharmony of the classes. He denied that one equals one, not only because everything that exists passes over ceaselessly and unremittingly into another and indeed into its opposite, but because in general nothing is identical with itself. Like every humorist he was especially interested in what becomes of things. You know the Berlin exclamation: "How you've changed, Emil! " [7] The cowardice of the brave and the bravery of the coward engaged him, in particular that everything contradicts itself, and especially the ups and downs, you understand—that everything goes forward very peacefully and leisurely and suddenly comes the crash. For him concepts were always rocking in a rocking-chair, something that makes a very good initial impression until it falls over backwards.

I once read his book, the "Larger Logic," as I had rheumatism and could not move myself. It is one of the most humorous works in world literature. It deals with the life of concepts, their slippery, unstable, irresponsible existence, how they revile each other and do battle with knives and then sit themselves down together at dinner as if nothing had happened. They appear, so to speak, in pairs; each is married to its opposite and they settle their affairs in pairs, that is, they sign contracts in pairs, enter into legal actions in pairs, contrive raids and burglaries in pairs, write books and give affidavits in pairs, and do so as pairs whose members are completely at odds with each other. What order affirms, disorder, its inseparable partner, opposes at once, in one breath where possible. They can neither live without one another nor with one another.

Kalle

Does the book deal only with such concepts?

Ziffel

Concepts *[Begriffe]* that one makes from something for oneself are very important. They are the handles *[Griffe]* with which one can move things. The book deals with how one can fit oneself in among the causes of the ongoing processes. For Hegel the point *[Witz]* of the thing was dialectic. Like all great humorists he brought out everything with a dead serious face. By the way where have you heard of him?

Kalle

In politics.

Ziffel

That is also one of his jokes *[Witze]*. The greatest rebels show themselves to be pupils of the greatest champion of the state. Besides, it speaks well for you that you have humor. I have never met a person without a sense of humor who has understood Hegel's dialectic.[8]

Without the sense of the incongruous, Hegel has no science. His dialectic depends upon the presence of humor within the reader's own existence. When consciousness takes itself seriously, it loses its flexibility. It freezes into the stance of only one of its possibilities and ceases its own worldly travel as a self. When the philosopher does this, it is the end of philosophy. Thought has no more life. In the circle of Hegelian science, each text has its keys. With them, the reader can make the truth of Hegel's concepts for himself. Each of Hegel's works demands a different approach. Metaphor, irony, and *Erinnerung* (the "absolute Muse") are the keys to Hegel's *Phänomenologie des Geistes*. These let us enter the "science of the experience of consciousness."

Appendix

Hegel's Titles and Contents

Below for ease of reference are the title, contents, and two internal title pages of Hegel's *Phenomenology,* in my translation. The Contents precedes the Preface, and the two internal title pages fall between the Preface and the Introduction. The first-edition copy of the *Phänomenologie des Geistes* I have seen in the Vatican Library includes a three-page list of *Verbesserungen* (printer's *corrigenda*) just before these internal title pages. No text of Hegel's title page or his internal title pages appears in either English translation of the *Phenomenology* (and the two internal title pages do not appear as such in Hoffmeister), but they are certainly important for Hegel's conception of his system.[1]

The title page and internal title pages leave the reader no doubt that Hegel intended his *Phenomenology of Spirit* to be the first part of a system of science, that such a phenomenology was itself a science, and that such a science was the "science of the experience of consciousness" *(Erfahrung des Bewusstseyns).*[2]

S Y S T E M

of

S C I E N C E

by

Ge. Wilh. Fr. Hegel

Dr. and Professor of Philosophy at Jena,
Associate of the Jena Ducal Mineralogical Society
and member of other learned associations.

First Part,

the

Phenomenology of Spirit.

Bramberg and Würzburg,
at Joseph Anton Goebhardt,
1807.

Hegel's two internal titles:

I.

Science

of the

Phenomenology

of

Spirit

First Part.

Science

of the

Experience

of

Consciousness

CONTENTS.

PREFACE: ON SCIENTIFIC KNOWING [ERKENNEN].

The element of the true is the concept and its true form scientific system—The present standpoint of spirit—The principle is not the completion, against formalism—The absolute is subject, and what this is—Element of knowing—The ascent to this is the phenomenology of spirit—Transformation of mental images and familiar ideas into thought, and this into the concept—To what extent the phenomenology of spirit is negative or contains the false—Historical truth and mathematical truth—Nature of philosophical truth and its method, against schematizing formalism—Requisite for the study of philosophy—Ratiocinative thought in its negative approach, in its positive; its subject—Natural philosophizing as common sense and as genius—Conclusion, relation of the writer to the public.

INTRODUCTION.

(A.) CONSCIOUSNESS.

(B.) SELF-CONSCIOUSNESS.

(C.) (AA.) REASON.

V. Certainty and Truth of Reason

A. Observational Reason

    a. Observation of nature

    Description in general, characteristics, laws

    Observation of the organic

        α. Relation of this to the inorganic— β. Teleology— γ. Inner and outer— αα. The inner—Laws of its pure moments, sensibility, etc.—The inner and its outer— ββ. The inner and the outer as concrete form— γγ. The outer itself as inner and outer or the organic idea carried over on to the inorganic—The organic from this side; its genus, species, and individuality.

    b. Observation of self-consciousness in its purity and its relation to external reality. Logical and psychological laws.

    c. In its relation to its immediate reality. Physiognomy, and Phrenology *[Schädellehre]*.

B. The Realization of Rational Self-consciousness through Itself

    a. Pleasure and necessity

    b. The law of the heart and the frenzy of self-conceit

    c. Virtue and the way of the world

C. Individuality, which in and for Itself is Real

    a. The spiritual animal kingdom and humbug or the matter in hand itself

    b. Law-giving reason

    c. Law-testing reason

(BB.) SPIRIT.

VI. Spirit

A. *True* Spirit. Customary Morality

    a. The world of customary morality. Human and divine law, man and woman

    b. Customary moral action. Human and divine knowing, guilt and destiny

    c. Legal status

B. *Self-estranged* Spirit. Culture

    I. The World of Self-estranged Spirit

        a. Culture and its realm of reality

        b. Faith and pure insight

    II. Enlightenment

        a. The battle of enlightenment with superstition

        b. The truth of enlightenment

    III. Absolute Freedom and Terror

C. *Self-certain* Spirit. Morality

    a. The moral world view

    b. Pretense

    c. Conscience. The beautiful soul, evil and its forgiveness

(CC.) RELIGION.

VII. *Religion*

A. *Natural* Religion

    a. Reality as light

    b. Plant and animal

    c. The artificer

B. *Art*-Religion

    a. The abstract art work

    b. The living art work

    c. The spiritual art work

C. *Revealed* Religion

(DD.) ABSOLUTE KNOWING.

VIII. Absolute Knowing

Notes

Chapter One: Introduction

1. M. J. Petry, *Hegel's Philosophy of Subjective Spirit*, 3 vols. (Dordrecht: Reidel, 1978), 1:lxxiii. Stanley Rosen holds that the *Logic* is *the* key to Hegel's thought; see *G. W. F. Hegel: An Introduction to the Science of Wisdom* (New Haven: Yale University Press, 1974), xiii.

2. Richard Kroner, "Introduction: Hegel's Philosophical Development," in *On Christianity: Early Theological Writings*, trans. T. M. Knox (New York: Harper Torchbooks, 1961), 46.

3. Johannes Hoffmeister, "Einleitung des Herausgebers," in G. W. F. Hegel, *Phänomenologie des Geistes*, ed. Johannes Hoffmeister (Hamburg: Meiner, 1952), vi.

4. *The Works of Aristotle*, ed. W. D. Ross, vol. 3, *Parva Naturalia* (Oxford: Clarendon Press, 1931), 449b–53b. Hegel refers to Aristotle's "De memoria et reminiscentia," see G. W. F. Hegel, *Sämtliche Werke. Jubiläumsausgabe*, ed. Hermann Glockner, 20 vols. (Stuttgart: Frommann, 1927–30), 18:369.

5. Ernst Bloch, "Zerstörte Sprache—zerstörte Kultur," in *Deutsche Literatur in Exil 1933–1945: Texte und Dokumente*, ed. Michael Winkler (Stuttgart: Reclam, 1979), 353–54. My translation. This was originally delivered as a lecture by Bloch in New York in 1939.

Cassirer quotes this last paragraph of the *Phenomenology* and stresses the importance of *Erinnerung* for the philosophy of culture, see *Symbol, Myth, and Culture: Essays and Lectures of Ernst Cassirer 1935–1945*, ed. Donald Phillip Verene (New Haven: Yale University Press, 1979), 79–80.

For another writer who is aware of the significance of Hegel's hyphenation of *Er-Innerung* see David Farrell Krell, "Der Maulwurf: Die philosophisches Wühlarbeit bei Kant, Hegel und Nietzsche (The Mole: Philosophic Burrowing in Kant, Hegel, and Nietzsche)," *Boundary 2: A Journal of Post-Modern Literature*, vol. 9, no. 3 and vol. 10, no. 1 (Spring/Fall 1981): 160, 166 n. 5, 174.

Cf. Dieter Henrich, *Hegel im Kontext* (Frankfurt am Main: Suhrkamp, 1975), 34 and Georg Lukács, *Der junge Hegel* (Zurich: Europa, 1948), 646.

6. Carl G. Vaught, *The Quest for Wholeness* (Albany: State University of New York Press, 1982), 176.

7. *Phänomenologie des Geistes,* ed. Hoffmeister, 563–64. My translation.

8. For a discussion of some of the features of this passage see Stephen Crites, "The Golgotha of Absolute Spirit," in *Method and Speculation in Hegel's Phenomenology,* ed. Merold Westphal (New Jersey and Sussex: Humanities Press and Harvester Press, 1982), 47–55.

9. For a literary analysis of Schiller's poem see Werner Keller, *Das Pathos in Schillers Jugendlyrik* (Berlin: Walter de Gruyter, 1964), 135–44. Cysarz's remark is from his *Schiller,* quoted by Keller, 136. See also, Emil Staiger, *Friedrich Schiller* (Zurich: Atlantis, 1967): 112–13.

10. Friedrich Schiller, *Sämtliche Werke,* ed. Gerhard Fricke and Herbert G. Göpfert in connection with Herbert Stubenrauch, 6th ed., 4 vols. (Munich: Hanser, 1974–80), 1:93. My translation.

11. G. W. F. Hegel, *Wissenschaft der Logik,* ed. Georg Lasson, 2 vols. (Hamburg: Meiner, 1971), 1:125–46.

12. Quentin Lauer, *A Reading of Hegel's Phenomenology of Spirit* (New York: Fordham University Press, 1976), 268.

13. G. W. F. Hegel, *Gesammelte Werke,* vol. 8, *Jenaer Systementwürfe III,* ed. Rolf-Peter Horstmann (Hamburg: Meiner, 1976), 187–90. My translation.

14. *Briefe von und an Hegel,* ed. Johannes Hoffmeister, 4 vols. (Hamburg: Meiner, 1952–60), 1:99–100.

15. On Hegel's views of the German language see Theodor Bodammer, *Hegels Deutung der Sprache: Interpretationen zu Hegels Äusserungen über die Sprache* (Hamburg: Meiner, 1969), 154–55 and Daniel J. Cook, *Language in the Philosophy of Hegel* (The Hague: Mouton, 1973), 66–70, 164–65, and 170.

16. Hoffmeister, "Einleitung," viii.

17. Ibid., xiii. My translation.

18. Ibid., xiv.

Chapter Two: The Method of In-itself

1. G. W. F. Hegel, *Phänomenologie des Geistes,* ed. Johannes Hoffmeister, 6th ed. (Hamburg: Meiner, 1952), 565.

Heidegger claims that: "The caption 'Introduction' does not appear in the original edition of 1807" (it appears not in the text but in the Contents), and that this section cannot really be an introduction "because there is no such thing as an introduction to phenomenology. The phenomenology of

Spirit is the *parousia* of the Absolute. The *parousia* is the Being of beings. There is for man no introduction to the Being of beings, because man's nature, his life led in the escort of Being, is itself that escort" (Martin Heidegger, *Hegel's Concept of Experience* [New York: Harper and Row, 1970], 150).

2. Gustav E. Mueller, "The Hegel Legend of 'Thesis-Antithesis-Synthesis'," *Journal of the History of Ideas* 19 (1958): 411–14. For a defense of the importance of triadic structure in Hegel's *Logic* see Philip W. Cummings, "Thesis-Antithesis-Synthesis: Legend or Fact? " *Journal of Critical Analysis* 6 (1976): 62–69. This is a criticism of Kaufmann's version of Mueller's thesis.

3. Mueller, 411.

4. George L. Kline, "Some Recent Reinterpretations of Hegel's Philosophy," *Monist* 48 (1964): 46–47.

5. W. T. Stace, *The Philosophy of Hegel: A Systematic Exposition* (1924; New York: Dover, 1955).

6. Mueller, 412.

7. R. G. Collingwood, *An Essay on Philosophical Method* (Oxford: Clarendon Press, 1933), pts. 2 and 3.

8. Descartes says in the *Discours:* "Those who have the strongest power of reasoning, and who most skillfully arrange their thoughts in order to render them clear and intelligible, have the best power of persuasion even if they can but speak the language of Lower Brittany *[bas breton]* and have never learned Rhetoric," *The Philosophical Works of Descartes,* trans. E. S. Haldane and G. R. T. Ross, 2 vols. (Cambridge: Cambridge University Press, 1931), 1:85.

Locke says in the *Essay:* "But yet if we would speak of things as they are, we must allow that all the art of rhetoric, besides order and clearness; all the artificial and figurative application of words eloquence hath invented, are for nothing else but to insinuate wrong ideas, move the passions, and thereby mislead the judgment; and so indeed are perfect cheats." *An Essay Concerning Human Understanding,* ed. A. C. Fraser, 2 vols. (Oxford: Clarendon Press, 1894), 2:146.

9. I am applying here Ernesto Grassi's view of the "primacy of rhetorical speech" to the interpretation of a stage of consciousness. See Ernesto Grassi, *Rhetoric as Philosophy: The Humanist Tradition* (University Park: The Pennsylvania State University Press, 1980), chap. 2.

10. Otto Pöggeler, "Hegel der Verfasser des ältesten Systemprogramms des deutschen Idealismus," *Hegel-Studien,* Beiheft 4 (1969): 17–32.

11. G. W. F. Hegel, "Das älteste Systemprogramm des deutschen Idealismus," *Werke,* 20 vols. (Frankfurt: Suhrkamp, 1971), 1:234–36. My translation. For a full English text of this fragment see H. S. Harris, *Hegel's Development: Toward the Sunlight 1770–1801* (Oxford: Clarendon Press, 1972), 510–12.

For an analysis from a rhetorical perspective of Hegel's early works see, John H. Smith, "The Spirit and Its Letter: The Rhetoric of Hegel's Early Writings," Ph.D. diss. (Princeton University, 1983).

12. On the question of the authorship of this piece, see *Mythologie der Vernunft Hegels "Ältestes Systemprogramm" des deutschen Idealismus,* ed. Christoph Jamme and Helmut Schneider (Frankfurt am Main: Suhrkamp, 1984).

Chapter Three: Das Meinen, *"Meaning"*

1. Shaftesbury, *"Sensus Communis:* An Essay on the Freedom of Wit and Humor," Treatise II of *Characteristics of Men, Manners, Opinions, Times,* ed. John M. Robertson (Indianapolis: Bobbs Merrill, 1964).

2. Andrea Battistini, "Antonomasia e universale fantastico," in *Retorica e critica letteraria,* ed. Lea Ritter Santini and Ezio Raimondi (Bologna: Società Editrice Il Mulino, 1978), 105–21.

3. Ernst Cassirer, *The Philosophy of Symbolic Forms,* vol. 2, *Mythical Thought,* trans. Ralph Manheim (New Haven: Yale University Press, 1955), xvi.

4. Hermann K. Usener, *Götternamen: Versuch einer Lehre von der religiösen Begriffsbildung* (Bonn: F. Cohen, 1896), chap. 16.

5. G. W. F. Hegel, *Gesammelte Werke,* vol. 8, *Jenaer Systementwürfe III,* ed. Rolf-Peter Horstmann (Hamburg: Meiner, 1976), 193.

6. Burton Feldman and Robert D. Richardson, *The Rise of Modern Mythology 1680–1860* (Bloomington: Indiana University Press, 1972), 302–48.

7. Ibid., 316 and xxv. It is significant that the editors of this comprehensive collection of materials on the modern study of mythology find no piece on myth from Hegel's works of sufficient length or specificity to include it as a selection.

8. William Chase Green, *Moira: Fate, Good, and Evil in Greek Thought* (Cambridge: Harvard University Press, 1944), 49–51.

9. The translation of this passage combines the Miller and Ballie translations.

10. Michael Grant, *Myths of the Greeks and Romans* (Cleveland and New York: Meridian Books, World Publishing Co., 1965), 144.

11. H. S. Harris, *Hegel's Development: Toward the Sunlight 1770–1801* (Oxford: Clarendon Press, 1972), 246.

12. Ibid.

13. This is one of a number of recently rediscovered manuscripts of Hegel. These manuscripts are referred to by Rosenkranz in *Hegel's Leben* (Berlin, 1844). For a description of the manuscripts see: Eva Ziesche, "Unbekannte Manuskripte aus der Jenaer und Nürnberger Zeit im Berliner Hegel-Nachlass," *Zeitschrift für philosophische Forschung* 29 (1975): 430–44.

The part of the text I have translated above is that quoted in Rosenkranz (180–81). It is corrected in one place to the original. I thank the Staatsbibliothek Preussischer Kulturbesitz in West Berlin and Frau Ziesche for her help in my transcription of the whole fragment. This manuscript and others are to appear in the new Meiner edition of Hegel's *Gesammelte Werke*.

14. Rosenkranz's quotation reads *oder*. The original manuscript reads *jeder*.

15. In this sentence Hegel is playing on the sense of *finding (Finden)* contained in the German word for invention *(Erfindung)*.

16. G. W. F. Hegel, *Werke,* 20 vols. (Frankfurt: Suhrkamp, 1971), 1:236. My translation.

Chapter Four: The Topsy-turvy World

1. J. N. Findlay, "Foreword," in *Phenomenology of Spirit,* trans. A. V. Miller (Oxford: Clarendon Press, 1977), xiii.

2. Hans-Georg Gadamer, "Die verkehrte Welt," *Hegel-Studien,* Beiheft 3 (1966): 135–54. English translation: Hans-Georg Gadamer, "Hegel's 'Inverted World'," in *Hegel's Dialectic: Five Hermeneutical Studies,* trans. P. Christopher Smith (New Haven: Yale University Press, 1976), 35–53. An English translation also appeared in *Review of Metaphysics* 28 (1975): 401–22.

Joseph C. Flay, "Hegel's 'Inverted World'," *Review of Metaphysics* 23 (1970): 662–78.

W. H. Bossart, "Hegel on the Inverted World" and Robert Zimmerman, "Hegel's 'Inverted World' Revisited," *The Philosophical Forum* 13 (1982) 326–41; 342–70. See also the comments on the inverted world, Martin J. De Nys, "Force and Understanding: the Unity of the Object of Consciousness," in *Method and Speculation in Hegel's Phenomenology,* ed. Merold Westphal (New Jersey and Sussex: Humanities Press and Harvester Press, 1982), 64–66; and M. J. Inwwod, "Solomon, Hegel, and Truth," *Review of Metaphysics* 31 (1977): 274–75.

Robert C. Solomon, *In the Spirit of Hegel: A Study of G. W. F. Hegel's Phenomenology of Spirit* (New York: Oxford University Press, 1983), 376–85. Solomon cites an unpublished manuscript that advances a theory of the inverted world: Jay Ogilvy, *Reading Hegel* (unpublished, 1974). See Solomon, 96n and 382n.

The *Hegel Bibliography/Bibliographie,* compiled by Kurt Steinhauer with keyword index by Gitta Hausen (Munich: Saur, 1980) under *Welt, verkehrte* lists only Gadamer's article and two of its German reprintings (omitting a third in *Hegel's Dialektik: Fünf hermeneutische Studien,* 1971, see entry no. 11138). Flay's article cannot be located through the keyword index. Such errors shake my confidence in the usefulness of this index.

Henry Sussman has given an intensive analysis of Hegel's chapter on Force and Understanding, including the role of the *verkehrte Welt,* employing methods of contemporary literary analysis in *The Hegelian Aftermath: Readings in Hegel, Kierkegaard, Freud, Proust, and James* (Baltimore: Johns Hopkins University Press, 1982), 33–49.

3. Descartes, *Meditations on First Philosophy,* 2d ed., trans. Laurence J. Lafleur (Indianapolis: Bobbs Merrill, 1960), 22.

4. Descartes, *Oeuvres,* ed. Adam and Tannery, 12 vols. (Paris, 1897–1910), 7:22, 9:17.

5. G. W. F. Hegel, *Sämtliche Werke: Jubiläumsausgabe,* ed. Hermann Glockner, 20 vols. (Stuttgart: Frommann, 1927–30), 19:331. My translation.

6. Ibid., 335. My translation.

7. Flay, 677.

8. Johannes Hoffmeister, "Einleitung des Herausgebers," in G. W. F. Hegel, *Phänomenologie des Geistes,* ed. Johannes Hoffmeister (Hamburg: Meiner, 1952), xiii–iv.

9. Flay, 662n.

10. Bossart, 326.

11. Gadamer, "Die verkehrte Welt," 135.

12. *Oxford English Dictionary,* s. v. "topsy-turvy."

13. Jean Hyppolite, *Genesis and Structure of Hegel's Phenomenology of Spirit,* trans. Samuel Cherniak and John Heckman (Evanston: Northwestern University Press, 1974), 136.

14. G. W. F. Hegel, *Wissenschaft der Logik,* ed. Georg Lasson, 2 vols. (Hamburg: Meiner, 1969), 2:310.

15. Aristotle, *Rhetoric* I. 1–2 and II. 20–23; *Prior Analytics* II. 27; *Topics,* I. 1.

16. G. W. F. Hegel, *Lectures on the History of Philosophy,* trans. E. S. Haldane and Frances H. Simson, 3 vols. (London: Kegan Paul, 1894), 2:217. Cf. the remarks on Aristotle's topics in Frances A. Yates, *The Art of Memory* (Chicago: University of Chicago Press, 1966), 31–35.

17. Ibid., 3:129

18. Walter Hinck, *Das deutsche Lustspiel des 17. und 18. Jahrhunderts und die italienische Komödie* (Stuttgart, 1965), 130. See also Klaus Lazarowicz, *Verkehrte Welt: Vorstudien zu einer Geschichte der deutschen Satire* (Tübingen, 1963).

19. *Komedia: Deutsche Lustspiele vom Barock bis zur Gegenwart. Texte und Materialien zur Interpretation,* No. 7, ed. Helmut Arntzen and Karl Pestalozzi (Berlin: Walter de Gruyter, 1964), 133. My translation.

20. *Bambocciaden,* ed. A. F. Bernhardi, zweiter Theil (Berlin: Friedrich Maurer, 1799), 103–276.

21. *Komedia,* 135.

22. Rudolf Haym, *Die romantische Schule: Ein Beitrag zur Geschichte des deutschen Geistes,* 2d ed. (Berlin: Weidmannsche Buchhandlung, 1906), 854–64, 892–94.

23. Edwin H. Zeydel, *Ludwig Tieck, The German Romanticist: A Critical Study* (Princeton: Princeton University Press, 1935), 128. Dilthey describes the heady atmosphere of Jena at this time. Wilhelm Dilthey, *Gesammelte Schriften,* vol. 4, *Die Jugendgeschichte Hegels* (Leipzig: Teubner, 1921), esp. 191–94.

24. G. W. F. Hegel, *Sämtliche Werke. Jubiläumsausgabe,* ed. Hermann Glockner, 20 vols. (Stuttgart: Frommann, 1927–30), 12:106. See also Sinclair's mention of F. Schlegel and Tieck in his letter to Hegel of 23 May 1807 in *Briefe von und an Hegel,* ed. Johannes Hoffmeister, 4 vols. (Hamburg: Meiner, 1952–60), 1:65.

25. *Wissenschaft der Logik,* 2:134. Hegel uses *Verkehrung* several times in the latter parts of the *Phenomenology* to describe dialectical movements within various moral standpoints, see, e.g., Hoffmeister, 271, 276, 346, 371–72, 375.

26. Ludwig Tieck, *Ludwig Tieck's Schriften,* 20 vols. (Berlin: Georg Reimer, 1828–46), 5:283–433.

27. Ludwig Tieck, *The Land of Upside Down,* trans. Oscar Mandel (London: Associated University Presses, 1978), 19.

28. Ibid.

29. Ibid.

30. Ibid., 20.

31. Mandel knows of no performance of the play except a student production of an abbreviated version done in Berlin in 1963 (ibid., 25). There was a production of Tieck's *Die verkehrte Welt* in the Schiller-Theater in Berlin, with a large cast and full program notes, which had its premiere December 22, 1975. I thank Dr. John Krois for giving me a copy of the program of this production.

32. Tieck, *Land of Upside Down,* 20.

33. Ibid., 121; *Tieck's Schriften,* 433.

34. Solomon says: "The 'curtain' metaphor, presumably, refers to the 'veil of Maya' of the Oriental mystics" (385n). Solomon, like all other commentators on this section, makes no mention of Tieck's play. Once the possibility is realized that Hegel is thinking of a stage play in connection with this section, the curtain *(Vorhang)* metaphor makes sense without the presumption that Hegel is indirectly and unexpectedly saying something about Oriental thought.

35. Gadamer, 135. See also Bossart, 326.

36. Quentin Lauer, *A Reading of Hegel's Phenomenology of Spirit* (New York: Fordham University Press, 1976), 83–84.

37. Gadamer, *Hegel-Studien,* 149, n. 13. Although Gadamer mentions the literary tradition, he does not mention Tieck's play.

38. Karl Rosenkranz, *Geschichte der deutschen Poesie im Mittelalter* (Halle, 1830), 586–94.

39. Sebastian Brant, *Narrenschiff*, ed. Friedrich Zarncke (Hildesheim: Olms, 1961). The better-known Latin text of Jacob Locher, entitled *Stultifera Navis*, appeared in 1497 (which Katherine Anne Porter mistook for the original text). For a modern English translation see *The Ship of Fools*, trans. Edwin H. Zeydel (New York: Columbia University Press, 1944). See also, Edwin H. Zeydel, *Sebastian Brant* (New York: Twayne, 1967).

40. Jacob and Wilhelm Grimm, *Deutsches Wörterbuch*, 16 vols. (Leipzig, 1854–1954), 12:1:630.

> Gar wenig worheyt man yetz hört
> Die heilig gschrifft würt vast verkört
> Und ander vil yetz usz geleitt
> Dann sie der munt der worheit seyt.

Narrenschiff, no. 103

> Eyn frow, die gern von wiszheit hört
> Die würt nit lycht jn schand verkört

Narrenschiff, no. 64

41. Gadamer, "Die verkehrte welt," 137. My translation.

42. Michel Foucault, *Madness and Civilization: A History of Insanity in the Age of Reason*, trans. Richard Howard (New York: Random House, Vintage Books, 1973), 7–8.

43. Ibid., 8.

44. Ibid., 11.

45. Rosenkranz, 594.

46. Johannes von Saaz, *The Plowman from Bohemia* (German and English opposed texts), trans. Alexander and Elizabeth Henderson (New York: Ungar, 1966), 103–4 (chap. 32). This is an even earlier (1401) use of *verkehren* than the *Narrenschiff* (1494).

47. Ibid., 49 (chap. 16).

48. William Willeford, *The Fool and His Scepter: A Study in Clowns and Jesters and Their Audience* (Evanston: Northwestern University Press, 1969), 92.

49. Rosenkranz, 592. My translation. The earliest senses of the fool contain the view that the fool is both negative and positive—that the fool's folly must be overcome and that the fool is himself a bearer of a special wisdom. In Erasmus's *Moriae Encominum* (1509) folly itself becomes a kind of wisdom.

50. Ibid. My translation.

51. Medard Boss, "Zollikoner Seminare," in *Erinnerung an Martin Heidegger,* ed. Günther Neske (Pfullingen: Neske, 1977), 31–45. English translation: "Martin Heidegger's Zollikon Seminars," trans. Brian Kenny, *Review of Existential Psychology and Psychiatry* 16 (1978–79): 7–20.

52. Medard Boss, the psychiatrist with whom Heidegger conducted seminars in Switzerland, reports that a dark shadow fell over Heidegger each day at ten o'clock. In response to Boss's question about it, Heidegger replied: "Always at this time of day 'das Denken' comes over me. Then, if I do not want to do myself painful violence, I have to surrender myself to it" (ibid., 8).

53. "Nur noch ein Gott kann uns Retten," *Der Spiegel,* 30 Jahrgang, Nr. 23 (31 May 1976): 3 *(Hausmitteilung)* and 193–219. This interview was done in September 1966, but at Heidegger's wish not published until his death. On the three-hundred-year waiting period see 212.

Chapter Five: Masterhood and Servitude

1. On the unified character of these three chapters of the *Phenomenology* see Merold Westphal, *History and Truth in Hegel's Phenomenology* (New Jersey and Sussex: Humanities and Harvester Press, 1978), chaps. 3 and 4. Although an interpretation different from my own, Westphal's exposition is most helpful.

2. *Immanuel Kant's Critique of Pure Reason,* trans. Norman Kemp Smith (London: Macmillan, 1958), A 235–36; B 294–95.

3. Ibid., A 293; B 349.

4. *The Philosophical Works of Descartes,* trans. Elizabeth S. Haldane and G. R. T. Ross, 2 vols. (Cambridge: Cambridge University Press, 1931), 1:85.

5. Ernesto Grassi, *Die Macht der Phantasie: Zur Geschichte abendländischen Denkens* (Köingstein/Ts.: Athenäum, 1979), 51. In Hegel see *Sämtliche Werke: Jubiläumsausgabe,* ed. Hermann Glockner, 20 vols. (Stuttgart: Frommann, 1927–30), 12:538.

See also Ernesto Grassi, "Hegels Missdeutung der lateinischen und humanistischen Tradition," *Praxis* 8 (1971): 109–27.

6. Grassi, *Phantasie,* 52. My translation.

7. Ernesto Grassi, *Rhetoric as Philosophy: The Humanist Tradition* (University Park: The Pennsylvania State University Press, 1980), chap. 2.

8. Karl Marx, *Early Writings,* trans. and ed. T. B. Bottomore (New York: McGraw-Hill, 1946), 198–99.

9. *Karl Marx: The Essential Writings,* ed. Frederic L. Bender (New York: Harper Torchbooks, 1972), 141.

10. Carl G. Vaught, *The Quest for Wholeness* (Albany: State University of New York Press, 1982), 177.

11. D. P. Verene, "Hegel's Account of War," in *Hegel's Political Philosophy*, ed. Z. A. Pelczynski (Cambridge: Cambridge University Press, 1971), 168–80.

12. Boethius, *The Consolation of Philosophy*, trans. James J. Buchanan (New York: Ungar, 1957), 1.

Chapter Six: The Unhappy Consciousness

1. Heinrich Wölfflin, *Principles of Art History: The Problem of the Development of Style in Later Art*, trans. M. D. Hottinger (London: G. Bell, 1932), 74.

2. Hegel's original text reads, *diese Ataraxie* (Hoffmeister, 156). This is lost in Miller's translation (see Miller, 205). Baillie employs untransliterated Greek.

3. G. W. F. Hegel, *The Philosophy of History*, trans. J. Sibree (New York: Dover, 1956), 392–93.

4. J. N. Findlay, *Hegel: A Re-Examination* (London: Allen and Unwin, 1958), 101.

5. Ibid.

6. On the interconnection between work and mental image (something overlooked by Marxism) see Ernesto Grassi, "Die Funktion der Arbeit und der Phantasie: das Problem," chap. 5, sec. 7 of *Humanismus und Marxismus: Zur Kritik der Verselbständigung von Wissenschaft* (Reinbeck: Rowohlt, 1973).

7. Nicholas of Cusa, *Of Learned Ignorance,* trans. Fr. Germain Heron (London: Routledge and Kegan Paul, 1954), 8–9.

8. Cassirer says of the concept of the absolute in Cusanus: "to speak with Hegel, whose basic thought Cusanus anticipates with remarkable clarity—knowledge could not set up the limit if it had not already transgressed it in some sense" (*The Individual and the Cosmos in Renaissance Philosophy*, trans. Mario Domandi [Oxford: Blackwell, 1963], 39).

9. Findlay, *Hegel,* 100.

10. G. W. F. Hegel, *Wissenschaft der Logik,* ed. Georg Lasson, 2 vols. (Hamburg: Meiner, 1969), 1:125.

Chapter Seven: Phrenology

1. J. N. Findlay, *Hegel: A Re-examination* (London: Allen and Unwin, 1958), 108.

2. In addition to MacIntyre's essay on Hegel's view of phrenology there is an eighty-seven page monograph, published twenty years after Hegel's death: Julius Schaller, *Die Phrenologie in ihren Grundzügen und nach ihrem wissenschaftlichen und praktischen Werthe* (Leipzig: Geibel, 1851).

3. Alasdair MacIntyre, "Hegel on Faces and Skulls," in *Hegel: A Collection of Critical Essays,* ed. Alasdair MacIntyre (Notre Dame: University of Notre Dame Press, 1976), 225.

4. Judith N. Shklar, *Freedom and Independence: A Study of the Political Ideas of Hegel's Phenomenology of Mind* (Cambridge: Cambridge University Press, 1976), 37–38.

5. John Caspar Lavater, *Essays on Physiognomy,* trans. (from French) Henry Hunter, 3 vols. in 5 (London: John Murray, 1792), 1:53 (frag. 10).

6. Graeme Tytler, *Physiognomy in the European Novel: Faces and Fortunes* (Princeton: Princeton University Press, 1982), 74.

7. On Lavater's own *Sprache* see Kamal Radwan, *Die Sprache Lavaters im Spiegel der Geistesgeschichte* [Munich Dissertation] (Göppingen: Alfred Kümmerle, 1972).

8. Tytler, 74–75.

9. B. F. Skinner, *Beyond Freedom and Dignity* (New York: Bantam/ Vintage Books), 22.

10. John D. Davies, *Phrenology: Fad and Science* (New Haven: Yale University Press, 1955), 7–8.

11. Cassirer, otherwise the most mild-mannered of philosophers, quotes this aggressive passage on skulls in a reply he drafted to an article written by the anti-Semite Bruno Bauch in the *Kant-Studien* (of which Bauch was co-editor with Hans Vaihinger) and to views he had expressed in *Der Panther.* Bauch says that he hopes an anthropologist will recognize his skull as German when after generations it is dug up ("Vom Begriff der Nation," *Kant-Studien* 21 [1917]: 141). Cassirer quotes Hegel's views to make clear what he thinks of such skulduggery. Cassirer's unpublished essay is forthcoming in a volume of *nachgelassene Schriften,* ed. John Michael Krois and Ernst Wolfgang Orth (Hamburg: Meiner, 1986).

12. In his remarks entitled "On the utterly absurd indecency of the Cynics" Augustine says: "They are the ones who not only wrap themselves in a cloak but also carry a club" (*The City of God against the Pagans,* trans. Philip Levine, 7 vols. [Cambridge: Harvard University Press, The Loeb Classical Library, 1966], 4:371).

Diogenes Laertius reports of the Cynic Diogenes:

"When someone first shook a beam at him and then shouted: 'Look out,' Diogenes struck the man with his staff and added, 'Look out.' "

"Once, Diogenes was asking alms of a bad-tempered man, who said, 'Yes, if you can persuade me.' 'If I could persuade you,' said Diogenes, 'I would persuade you to hang yourself.' "

"Once when found behaving indecently in public [in fact, publicly mas-
turbating], he wished, 'It were as easy to banish hunger by rubbing the
belly.' "

"Asked why people give to beggars but not to philosophers, he said,
'Because they think they may one day be lame or blind but never expect
to become philosophers' " (*Lives of the Philosophers,* trans. A. Robert Caponigri
[Chicago: Henry Regnery, 1969], 144–49).

13. George Berkeley, *Three Dialogues Between Hylas and Philonous,* ed.
Colin M. Turbayne (Indianapolis: Bobbs Merrill, 1954), 52.

14. Gilbert Ryle, *The Concept of Mind* (New York: Barnes and Noble,
1949), 328.

15. These are no different than what can be found in O. S. and L. N.
Fowler, *The Self-Instructor in Phrenology and Physiology: with over one
hundred new illustrations, including a chart for the use of practical phrenologists*
(New York: Fowler and Wells, 1890). The title page bears the statement:
"Self-knowledge is the essence of *all* knowledge. Your character corresponds
with your organization."

16. Davies, 8; see also Tytler, 93.

17. Nahum Capen, "Biography of Dr. Gall," in François Joseph Gall,
On The Origin of the Moral Qualities and Intellectual Faculties of Man,
trans. Winslow Lewis, 6 vols. (Boston: Marsh, Capen, and Lyon, 1835),
1:19.

18. Ibid., 1:21.

Chapter Eight: Two Forms of Defective Selfhood

1. J. N. Findlay, *Hegel: A Re-examination* (London: Allen and Unwin,
1958), 113.

2. Martin Heidegger, *An Introduction to Metaphysics,* trans. Ralph Manheim (New Haven: Yale University Press, 1959), 166. The German text
reads: "Was heute vollends als Philosophie des Nationalsozialismus her-
umgeboten wird, aber mit der inneren Wahrheit und Grösse dieser Bewegung (nämlich mit der Begegnung der planetarisch bestimmten Technik
und des neuzeitlichen Menschen) nicht das Geringste zu tun hat, das macht
seine Fischzüge in diesen trüben Gewässern der 'Werte' und der 'Ganz-
heiten' " (*Einführung in die Metaphysik* [Tübingen: Niemeyer, 1953], 152).

3. Ernst Cassirer, "The Technique of Our Modern Political Myths,"
in *Symbol, Myth, and Culture: Essays and Lectures of Ernst Cassirer 1935–1945,*
ed. Donald Phillip Verene (New Haven: Yale University Press, 1979), 253.
See also two other essays of Cassirer in this volume, "Philosophy and

Politics" (219–32) and "Judaism and the Modern Political Myths" (233–41); and *The Myth of the State* (New Haven: Yale University Press, 1946).

4. Herbert Marcuse, *One-Dimensional Man: Studies in the Ideology of Advanced Industrial Society* (Boston: Beacon Press, 1964), xvi.

5. Karl Jaspers, *Man in the Modern Age,* trans. Eden and Cedar Paul (New York: Doubleday Anchor Books, 1957), 123.

6. Jacques Ellul, *The Technological Society,* trans. John Wilkinson (New York: Knopf, 1964; orig. French ed., 1954), 80. See also Ellul's sequel to this work, *The Technological System,* trans. Joachim Neugroschel (New York: Continuum, 1980; orig. French ed., 1977).

Concerning the connection between Ellul's and Hegel's ideas see Donald Phillip Verene, "Technological Desire," in vol. 7 of *Research in Philosophy and Technology,* ed. Paul T. Durbin (Greenwich, Conn.: JAI Press, 1984).

7. Ellul, *Technological Society,* 97.

8. Ibid., 74.

9. H. S. Harris, *Hegel's Development: Toward the Sunlight 1770–1801* (Oxford: Clarendon Press, 1972), xxviii.

10. Benjamin C. Sax, "Active Individuality and the Language of Confession: The Figure of the Beautiful Soul in the *Lehrjahre* and the *Phänomenologie,*" *Journal of the History of Philosophy* 21 (1983): 441.

11. Novalis, "Aufzeichnungen zum Heinrich von Ofterdingen," *Werke und Briefe* (Munich: Winkler, 1968), 306. My translation.

Chapter Nine: Religion versus Absolute Knowing

1. Merold Westphal, *History and Truth in Hegel's Phenomenology* (New Jersey and Sussex: Humanities Press and Harvester Press, 1976), 211.

2. Alexandre Kojève, *Introduction to the Reading of Hegel: Lectures on the Phenomenology of Spirit,* trans. James H. Nichols, Jr. (New York: Basic Books, 1969), 75.

3. Ibid., 75–76.

4. J. N. Findlay, *Hegel: A Re-examination* (London: Allen and Unwin, 1958): 146–47.

5. "Vacuous actuality" is Whitehead's term. See Alfred North Whitehead, *Process and Reality: An Essay in Cosmology* (New York: Harper Torchbooks, 1960), 43. Whitehead says: "The difficulties of all schools of modern philosophy lie in the fact that, having accepted the subjectivist principle, they continue to use philosophical categories derived from another point of view. . . . They have generated two misconceptions: *one* is the concept of vacuous actuality, void of subjective experience" (253).

Chapter Ten: Epilogue

1. G. W. F. Hegel, *Wissenschaft der Logik,* ed. Georg Lasson, 2 vols. (Hamburg: Meiner, 1971), 1:7. *Hegel's Science of Logic,* trans. A. V. Miller (London: Allen and Unwin, 1969), 29.

2. *Logik,* 2:505; *Logic,* 843.

3. *Logik,* 2:504; *Logic,* 842.

4. *Logik,* 2:505; *Logic,* 843. Vittorio Mathieu has argued that there is no question of Hegel imposing dialectical structure on nature from the *Logic,* because Hegel has already established from his earlier examination of nature that it has dialectical structure. See his excellent essay, "Filosofia della natura e dialettica," in *Hegel interprete di Kant,* ed. Valerio Verra (Naples: Prismi, 1981), 91–122.

5. Carl G. Vaught, *The Quest for Wholeness* (Albany: State University of New York Press, 1982), 184.

6. G. W. F. Hegel, "Wer denkt abstrakt?," *Werke,* 20 vols. (Frankfurt am Main: Suhrkamp, 1970), 2:575–81. English trans.: Walter Kaufmann, "Who Thinks Abstractly?" in *Hegel: Reinterpretation, Texts, and Commentary* (New York: Doubleday, 1965), 461–65.

7. Brecht seems to have in mind the following ironic remark, made on visiting the gravesite of a friend and finding a large flower growing from it: "My, how you've changed, my friend!" This can be found in a folk poem in Berlin dialect entitled "Die Seelenwanderung" (The transmigration of souls) that is an exchange between "Zwei kleine Knaben, Fritz und Karl/zwei richtige berlinger Jungen." The last lines of this poem are:

> Da liegste nu uff grüner Au
> von grünem Rasen zart umrändert.
> Und ick denk wehmutsvoll und still:
> Mensch Karl, wie haste Dir verändert.

8. Bertolt Brecht, *Flüchtlingsgespräche* (Berlin and Frankfurt: Suhrkamp, 1961), 108–111. My translation. Brecht's work was written in Finland in 1941 and published posthumously.

Appendix: Hegel's Titles and Contents

1. For details of the title pages, see the editorial comments in G. W. F. Hegel, *Gesammelte Werke,* vol. 5, *Phänomenologie des Geistes,* ed. Wolf-

gang Bonsiepen and Reinhard Heede (Hamburg: Meiner, 1980), 51, 444, 469, and 455.

2. The second internal title page, announcing the "science of the experience of consciousness," did not appear in all copies of the first edition. See ibid., 469.

Index

Capen, Nahum, 88
Caput mortuum, 85, 89
Cassirer, Ernst, 31, 94, 137n.11
Ceres, 33
Chalybäus, Heinrich Mortiz, 19
Cicero, 48
"Circle of circles," 108, 113, 116–17, 120
Cogito, 39, 42–43
Coincidentia oppositorum, 76
Collingwood, R. G., 23
Commedia dell'arte, 50
Concept. *See Begriff*
Concept of Mind, The, 86
Consolation of Philosophy, The, 68
Cusanus. *See* Nicholas of Cusa
Cysarz, Herbert, 6

Dance of Death. *See Totentanz*
Death, 59, 67–68. *See also Totentanz*
Demeter, 35, 38, 45
Denken, das, 57, 135
Descartes, René, 19, 41–43, 56, 61, 82, 93, 129n.8
Desire, 59, 62
Diogenes, 85, 137–38n.12
Discours de la méthode, 19, 61, 129
Docta ignorantia, 119

Economic and Philosophical Manuscripts, 66
Eichendorff, Joseph Freiherr von, 50
Einführung in die Metaphysik, 93
Electricity, 44, 47, 51
Eleusinian mysteries, 28, 33, 35–36, 45
Ellul, Jacques, 96–97
Entsprechen, 27, 60–61, 70, 108; meaning of the term, 17

Epictetus, 71, 73
Erfahrung, 10, 16, 28, 108
Erinnerung: hyphenation of the term, 3–5. *See also* Recollection
Euripides, 33
Existentialism, 95–96

Ferguson, Adam, 6
Findlay, John, x, 39–40, 72, 77, 80, 93
Flay, Joseph C., 40, 43, 51
Flüchtlingsgespräche, 119
Fools. *See Narrenschiff*
Forgetting, 29, 35, 38, 75, 79, 107, 109–10
Foucault, Michel, 54
"Freundschaft, Die," 6
Friendship, 6–7, 13, 25

Gadamer, Hans-Georg, 40, 43, 51–53
Galerie von Bildern, x, 4, 22, 37
Galileo Galilei, 51
Gall, Franz Joseph, 80, 82–83, 88
Geschichte der deutschen Poesie im Mittelalter, 53
Gesunder Menschenverstand, 32, 52
Gleich: meaning of the term, 17–18
Goethe, Johann Wolfgang von, 32, 100
Götternamen, 31
Grassi, Ernesto, x, 65
Green, William Chase, 33
Grimm, William, 50
Grimm's *Deutsches Wörterbuch,* 53

Harris, H. S., 36, 100
Hegel: A Re-examination, x
"Hegel as Poet," x